THE FOUR GOSPELS AND ACTS A Short Introduction

by

HARRY R. BOER

GRAND RAPIDS

WILLIAM B. EERDMANS PUBLISHING COMPANY

Copyright © 1982 by Wm. B. Eerdmans Publishing Company
255 Jefferson Ave., S.E., Grand Rapids, MI 49503

Library of Congress Cataloging in Publication Data

Boer, Harry R.
The four Gospels and Acts.

   1. Bible. N.T. Gospels—Criticism, interpretation,
etc. 2. Bible. N.T. Acts—Criticism, interpretation,
etc. I. Title.
BS2548.B63   226'.06   82-1560
ISBN 0-8028-1901-X (pbk.)   AACR2

CONTENTS

I	THE GOSPEL AND THE GOSPELS	1
II	PALESTINE AT THE TIME OF JESUS	6
III	MATTHEW	12
IV	MARK	23
V	LUKE	33
VI	HIGHER CRITICISM	44
VII	THE SYNOPTIC PROBLEM	53
VIII	JOHN	64
IX	THE ROMAN WORLD	84
X	THE ACTS OF THE APOSTLES	90

THE FOUR GOSPELS
AND
ACTS A Short Introduction

CHAPTER I

THE GOSPEL AND THE GOSPELS

It will be well to begin this book with a comment on the word "introduction" in its title. When we are introduced to a person the way is open to become acquainted with him. We can also be introduced to books. A book is in many ways like a person. We meet in its pages the thoughts and, in varying degrees, the personality of the author.

In the great area of literature the Bible stands out as *the Book* among the books. It introduces us not only to the thoughts of men but also to those of God himself as he speaks to us through men. The New Testament portion of the Bible begins with five short pieces of writing, and it is with these pieces that the present book is concerned. Four of them are called gospels; they describe the earthly ministry of Jesus. The fifth is known as the Acts of the Apostles. It traces the continuing ministry of Jesus through the Holy Spirit in the fundamentally important earliest years of the church's life. The purpose of this book is to introduce the reader to these five basic writings.

The chapters that follow will give some idea of the authorship, purpose, characteristics, structure, content, and other features of each of the four gospels and Acts. We hope the meeting of the reader with these books will lead him or her into friendship with them and understanding of them. It will be useful, however, first to meet the four gospels as a group. Matthew, Mark, Luke, and John are like brothers, each of whom has his own distinct personality, but who together also show family traits and qualities that they have in common. It is very important to see this. There is only one gospel of our Lord and Savior Jesus Christ. We must therefore understand correctly what we are saying when we speak of "the four gospels." It is necessary to note the difference between the *four* gospels as *books* and the *one* gospel as the *message of salvation*. It must be clear in our minds that the gospel existed before the gospels were written.

1. Let us begin by considering the word "gospel." It is derived from the old English word "godspell," which is a combination of

two words, "god" and "spell." In very early English "good" was spelled "god" and the word for "news" was "spell." The present word "gospel" is, therefore, a descendant of "godspell," meaning "good news." It is a direct translation of the Greek word *euangelion*, which is in turn a combination of the two words *eu* and *angelion*, meaning good and message respectively. From it come the familiar English words evangelist, evangel, evangelism, evangelical, and evangelize.

2. In the Greek New Testament the word *euangelion* is used some seventy-five times. It always refers to a message, never to a book. The message that it refers to is the joyful report of salvation through Jesus Christ; it is good news, revelation from God, the subject of preaching and teaching. We should be aware of this when we use expressions like "a gospel," "the gospels," "the gospel of John," "Mark's gospel," and so forth. It is not wrong to use these expressions as a matter of convenience. But we should always remember that first generation Christians did not know of such a use of the word "gospel."

When Mark speaks of "the beginning of the gospel of Jesus Christ" (1:1), he does not refer to the book that he is writing; rather, he refers to the beginning or origin of the message concerning Jesus Christ. Luke speaks of those who have undertaken to write "a narrative" of the things that had happened with respect to Jesus, and he now writes to Theophilus to give him an orderly account of them (1:1, 3). That is as close as Luke came to giving his book a title. Far from speaking about four gospels, therefore, the early church spoke only of "the gospel." It did so even when it named the books that we now call gospels, for it gave every one of them the title "the gospel." In order to distinguish between the four, however, it designated the one gospel concerning which all had written by the words "according to Matthew," "according to Mark," and so forth. Each man wrote a different book, but all were concerned with the one and only gospel of salvation.

In discussions with those who do not know the good news concerning Christ, we should therefore be careful how we use the expression "the four gospels." We should exercise this care especially when we speak with Muslims, Hindus, and members of other non-Christian communities. We should also point out to them that there are many other reports about the one gospel in the New Testament. Twenty-one of these are letters of St. Paul and other writers, one is a historical book named the Acts of the Apostles, and one is a prophecy concerning the End-time named Revelation. Acts serves as a transition between the four gospels and the rest of the New Testament. It narrates the *continuation* of "all that Jesus began to do and teach" (1:1) in the gospels. It relates the coming into being of the church, with whose life and witness the letters and the Revelation are concerned.

3. There is a further matter to note about the fact that the one gospel about the words and deeds of Jesus has been described in four accounts. Each of the four books has something to say that the others do not say or do not say so clearly or so fully. The church accepted them as genuine and authoritative at an early date. At the same time, it rejected a notable effort to unite the four gospels into one account. About A.D. 180 a certain Christian named Tatian, probably a Syrian, combined the four gospels by selecting passages from each, skillfully weaving them into one continuous narrative. The following passage is an example of his work:

And the servants and the soldiers rose, and made	Jo. 18:18
a fire in the middle of the court, that they	Lu. 22:55
might warm themselves, for it was cold. And Simon	
also came and sat down with them to warm himself	Jo. 18:18ᶜ
that he might see the end of what should happen.	Mt. 26:58ᶜ

This narrative was called the *Diatessaron*, a Greek word which means "the Fourfold." For a while Syriac-speaking churches accepted it as canonical. When the church as a whole officially defined the Canon of the New Testament (in 367 and again in 397), however, the Syrian churches rejected the *Diatessaron* and in time it disappeared from the usage of the church.

4. On the surface, the gospels appear to be biographies of Jesus. It would be a serious mistake, however, to describe the gospels as presenting the story of Jesus' life. For example, Mark and John do not say a word about the first thirty years of Jesus' life; Matthew and Luke relate the birth of Jesus, and Luke adds an incident in Jesus' twelfth year. The first thirty years in a man's life are extremely important in determining what kind of person he will be from age thirty on. Yet we know virtually nothing about that long span of years in Jesus' life. We read only that he was obedient to his parents and increased in wisdom and in stature, and was in favor with God and man (Luke 2:51, 52).

Furthermore, while the reports about Jesus' ministry say many things about him, we do not have the full story of his ministry. About a third of the chapters that deal with Jesus' ministry are concerned with the last few weeks of his life. In John, chapters twelve to twenty speak only of his last nine or ten days. It is clear, then, that

Jesus' death had as much meaning for the disciples as did his life. Moreover, every one of the gospels except Mark* gives great prominence to the resurrection. Earlier chapters deal with Jesus' preaching and healing ministry. All other concerns are passed over or stand in the background.

The gospels, therefore, do not at all present the life story of Jesus. Rather, they have a quite different purpose: they present a message. That message has a name. It is the *euangelion*, the gospel, the good news. In Jesus the kingdom of God came among men. In his teaching and in his life he explained and demonstrated the meaning and purpose of the kingdom. In his arrest, crucifixion, and death he showed the meaning of obedience in that kingdom. In his resurrection he conquered death and all the powers of evil. That is the one gospel that the four gospels tell. It is news that invites men to believe:

> Now Jesus did many other things in the presence of his disciples, which are not written in this book; but these are written that you may believe that Jesus is the Christ, the Son of God, and that believing you may have life in his name (John 20:30–31).

5. A word should be spoken about the reason for the writing of the gospels. The time in which they were written (between A.D. 65 and 95) was also the time in which the eyewitnesses of Jesus' ministry, notably the apostles, were passing away. As a message about Jesus and his work, the gospel had been preserved in the form of oral tradition. It was very desirable that an authoritative written account of this tradition be preserved. The apostles had been closer to Jesus than any others; they were the interpreters of his words and deeds. To them he had given authority to speak in his name. Furthermore, the leadership of the churches was in their hands. Therefore, a truly authoritative account of Jesus' ministry, suffering, death, and resurrection should be apostolic in character. The church considered that such an account was given by Matthew and John directly, by Mark through his association with both Peter and Paul, and by Luke through his association with Paul. They were placed first in the New Testament doubtless because the whole of the gospel arises out of what they spoke about—the incarnation, ministry, death, and resurrection of the Lord Jesus Christ.

The first century of our reckoning of time A.D. began with the birth of Jesus. At the one-third way point in the first century his work was accomplished. By A.D. 66, the two-thirds way point, the

---

*For the probable reason cf. Chapter IV, point 10 under Characteristics.

church was an established fact, the worldwide preaching of the gospel had been begun, and Paul's career as the greatest of church founders had come to an end. In the course of the last third of the century, A.D. 66–100, the four gospels were written. It is worthy of note that there is no period in the history of the church about which we know so little as of these years. They are almost a blank. It is the more remarkable therefore that it is in the course of these years that the gospels were written.

6. Finally, we must take note of the fact that the four gospels are rather clearly divided into two parts. The first part consists of Matthew, Mark, and Luke. There is between them a remarkable similarity expressing itself in many ways. They have therefore been called the Synoptics, a name derived from a Greek word meaning "to-see-things-together." We shall refer to them by this name again and again. At the same time, there are many dissimilarities between them. The difficulties created by this unusual combination of similarity and dissimilarity in the first three gospels are known as the Synoptic Problem. We shall devote a separate chapter to discussing it.

Meanwhile, we have John standing in a class by himself. He has few of the features that relate the Synoptics to each other so closely. Moreover, he has a style of writing and a theological manner of setting forth the good news of Christ that is quite distinct from Matthew-Mark-Luke.

This striking diversity in the gospels is not a sign of division or disagreement among them but rather of their unity. Together they set forth the riches, the depth, and the beauty of the one unchanging gospel of our Lord and Savior Jesus Christ.

CHAPTER II

PALESTINE AT THE TIME OF JESUS

The story that is told in the four gospels unfolds in its entirety in the country named Palestine. Its central figure is Jesus the Messiah. In him God's concern with Israel comes to its climax. Matthew especially emphasizes this. In doing so, he as well as Mark, Luke, and John indicate directly and indirectly the close relationship of their accounts to the earlier religion and life of Israel. The history from Abraham to Jesus is continuous, and we must take brief note of it. The four gospels cannot be appreciated properly without some knowledge of this history.

The larger part of Israel's history is well known in the church, and we shall refer to it here only in broad lines. God called Abraham to become the father of a separate people. This call was attended by two major promises: God would give Abraham many descendants, and he would also give them a separate land in which they would live. These two promises were confirmed to his son Isaac, and again to Jacob the son of Isaac and father of the twelve patriarchs of Israel. Meanwhile, Abraham, Isaac, and Jacob lived as wanderers in Canaan—the future homeland of their descendants. Driven by famine, the twelve sons of Jacob went to live in Egypt. There they became a numerous people, but eventually were enslaved by Pharaoh. Responding to their cry, God raised up Moses, a great leader and lawmaker who led them out of bondage into freedom.

Their release from bondage and escape from Egypt profoundly impressed the Israelites, who gave it a name: the Exodus (the way out). The Ten Commandments given to Moses in the course of Israel's desert wanderings begin with a recollection of the Exodus: "I am the Lord thy God who brought thee out of the land of Egypt, out of the house of bondage." After forty years of desert journeying and camping the Israelites conquered Canaan and settled in the promised land. Common descent from Abraham, the Exodus as deliverance from slavery, the Law to govern a life of gratitude to God for deliverance granted, and a land in which to live—these are foundational realities in the history of Israel.

The conquest of Canaan climaxed in united nationhood under

the kingship of David, and Israel became for a while a powerful nation. But after the death of Solomon, his son and successor, the united nation split into the northern and southern kingdoms about 920 B.C. The smaller southern kingdom remained loyal to the House of David, but the northern section chose its own king. In 722 the northern kingdom was conquered by the Assyrians who carried many of its leading people into exile. In 596 and later the more influential part of the population of Judah was similarly taken into exile by the Babylonians. About 536 B.C., under the sponsorship of Cyrus, the king of the Persians who had conquered Babylon, many returned to their native land. A hundred years later other groups returned under the leadership of Zerubbabel and Ezra. The Jews rebuilt the temple, which the Babylonians had destroyed, and continued their distinctive religious life in their ancient homeland.

From this point on the history of Israel is not at all familiar to most Christians. The 350 or so years intervening between Old and New Testament history were, however, extremely significant in shaping the people, the religion, and the history of the Jewish community that we meet in the four gospels and Acts. We must therefore pay somewhat more extended attention to this period.

Palestine remained under Persian control until 333 B.C. In that year Asia Minor, Syria, Palestine, and Egypt came under the control of Alexander, king of Macedonia (today the northern part of Greece), who is known in history as Alexander the Great. He had inherited the kingdom in 335. In 334 he conquered all of Greece and then moved eastward to conquer the whole of the vast area lying between Asia Minor and the western boundary of India. He died in 323 when he was only thirty-three years old.

The great empire that Alexander had created fell apart as his generals fought over and divided it. Palestine fell under the political control of Egypt, which was governed by one of Alexander's generals named Ptolemy. Syria, lying north of Palestine, had come under the control of another general named Seleucis. From time to time the Seleucid kings challenged the control of the Ptolemies, and in 198 B.C. they succeeded in incorporating Palestine into their domain. The effect that this change of government had on the Jews was profound.

The Ptolemies had been tolerant toward the Jewish people, and had allowed them full freedom to lead their life and practice their religion as they wished. The Seleucids, on the other hand, began to take this freedom from them. The new rulers considered Jewish culture and religion to be a hindrance to their own cultural, religious, and political aims. They began to impose Greek culture and Greek religion on the Jewish people. They desecrated the temple, forced the Jews to eat swine's flesh, forbade circumcision, and cruelly persecuted those who would not submit to the new way of life.

By 167 the Jews were ripe for revolt. It began with a priest named Mattathias who refused to obey the order of a representative of the king to sacrifice to the Greek god Zeus. He killed both the Jew who undertook to sacrifice in his stead and the officer who had ordered it, and he destroyed the altar. He then fled to the mountains with his family and from there organized a revolt against the Seleucid ruler.

Mattathias died in 166, but his sons continued the struggle. It was led with great success by Judas, who is better known as Judas Maccabeus (which means Judas the Hammer). National independence was achieved in 142 and lasted until 63. In that year political and religious dissension among the Jews led the opposing parties to appeal to Rome for support. Rome intervened, and from that time on Palestine's rulers were Roman appointees. The Jews were no longer masters in their own house.

Among these appointees was Antipater, an Idumean or Edomite who had become a convert to Judaism. He was a favorite of the imperial authorities in Rome, but the Jews were unhappy that an Edomite was their governor. As the chief political power in Palestine, Antipater secured for his son Herod the governorship of Galilee. On the death of his father in 43 B.C. Herod succeeded him, and in 39 the Roman senate appointed him to be king. In 6 B.C. Palestine officially became a Roman province. It was probably two years later, the last year of Herod's life, that Jesus was born (Matt. 2:1; Luke 1:5). Pontius Pilate was the Roman procurator of Judea from A.D. 26 to 36. In his administration Jesus was arrested and executed by crucifixion.

In spite of all their troubles and changes in political authority, the Jews maintained their identity, no small part of which was their religious character. Its central focus was the rebuilt temple in Jerusalem, which had been greatly enlarged by Herod. In all other areas the local center of religion was the synagogue. This unique Jewish institution probably originated in the exile as a substitute for the destroyed temple. It is in any case certain that it was during the exile that Jewish worship acquired the distinctive synagogal character that is so often alluded to in the gospels and in Acts. Its leading officer was the president of the meeting, who is usually referred to in the New Testament as the ruler of the synagogue. Under him functioned a helper to lead in congregational prayer, and still another to read the Scriptures. A third officer had custody of the Scriptures and functioned as president of the assembly in the absence of the ruler.

Another institution of great importance in the time of Jesus was the Sanhedrin, a council of seventy-one members that, under the Roman procurators, governed the whole of Palestine. The extent of its authority varied from time to time, but as a rule it had the power to make laws, to enforce them, and to act judicially in disputes. It governed the whole of Jewish life, civil as well as religious. In addition, it had authority not only among Jews in the homeland, but also over the Dispersion, the Jews who lived scattered or dispersed outside of Palestine. In the New Testament the Sanhedrin is also called "the council" or "the council of the elders." Its president was the High Priest—who was no longer of the priestly house of Aaron but an appointee of the Roman government. That the High Priest was president of the Sanhedrin indicates how indivisible religious and civil life were in Israel's community.

Geographically, Palestine was divided by the Jordan River. It separated Judea, Samaria, and Galilee on the western side from Peraea and Decapolis on the eastern. North of these eastern districts lay an area under the authority of Philip, Herod's son. Nearly the whole of Jesus' ministry was performed on the western side of the Jordan. There Jewish Judea in the south and Jewish Galilee in the north were divided by the area or district known as Samaria. References to Samaria and Samaritans in Luke, John, and Acts are not frequent, but they are significant. A word about Samaria is therefore in order.

Samaritans did not consider themselves to be Jews, and a great deal of hostility existed between them and the Jews. There were two major reasons for this hostility. First of all, the wounds created by the separation of the ten northern tribes from Judea and Benjamin in the south never healed entirely. In the second place, developments after 722 B.C. deepened the animosity. In that year the Assyrians conquered the northern kingdom and took many Israelites into exile. In their place they settled pagans from other countries that they had conquered (II Kings 17:24–41). These pagans not only brought their own religion with them, but they influenced the Samaritans among whom they dwelt. In turn the newcomers were influenced by the religion of the Samaritans. Thus Israelites (of the northern kingdom) lived alongside the pagan elements for 600 years prior to the coming of Christ. During these six centuries social and religious interchange brought into being a religious mixture that may be called the Samaritan religion. It consisted of a complex of beliefs that were, however, more Jewish than pagan: 1) belief in God, 2) acceptance of Moses as the chief prophet of God, 3) acceptance of the Pentateuch as the only revelation from God, 4) worship in Mt. Gerizim (cf. Deut. 11:29; 27:12), and 5) expectation of final judgment. In spite of this watering down of the Old Testament witness, the book of Acts reports substantial response to the gospel in Samaria (8:4–8, 25).

There were four classes of men who played an important role in Jewish religious life. They were the priests, the sadducees, the pharisees, and the scribes. At the head of the Jewish priesthood stood the High Priest. He was, as already noted, far more than simply a religious figure. When the Davidic line ceased to function during and after the exile, the High Priest gained greatly in influence and prestige. On return from the exile he became the civil as well as the religious head of the Jewish people. His power was diminished when the Herodian house provided kings, but he remained a powerful figure in all national affairs.

The priests served under the supervision of the High Priest. They were custodians of the sacred vessels and performed the necessary sacrifices. At the time of Jesus the priesthood was divided into twenty-four divisions or courses that served a week at a time (cf. Luke 1:8, 9, 23). The priests were also teachers of the law and the traditions. In New Testament times, however, this aspect of priestly service had moved into the background because of the importance that the pharisees had achieved as teachers of the law.

The sadducees must be discussed in connection with the priests because they were a special kind of priest. They were particularly concerned with the study and teaching of the law. Their name is probably derived from Zadok who was High Priest under king Solomon. For many generations the house of Zadok provided the high priests and also many of the priests in and around Jerusalem (although men with ancestry other than that of Zadok could also become priests and sadducees). In addition to their interest in the law, the sadducees were very interested in political affairs. They formed a sort of religious-political party in Israel that had been very influential, but which in New Testament times was overshadowed by the pharisees.

The sadducees accepted only the five books of Moses (i.e., the Pentateuch) as authoritative. In contrast, the pharisees accepted also the Prophets and the Writings, that is, the entire Old Testament as we now know it. For the sadducees all things taught in the Prophets and the Writings might or might not be true. They did not therefore have final authority. This was reserved only for the books of the Pentateuch.

The pharisees were lay teachers of the law. They were not involved therefore in the priesthood or in the work of the temple. During the exile the law had replaced the temple as the center of Jewish life. It was taught in the synagogues, and this body of lay teachers grew up to become expert in this instruction. The name "pharisee" probably comes from a Hebrew word meaning "separate" to indicate religious purity and separation from the common life of the people. The spiritual father of the pharisees was Ezra, who upon his return from the exile gave a special place to the law in the life of Israel.

The pharisees were anti-Roman in their political outlook but they were, on the whole, more devout than the strongly politically minded sadducees. The major emphases in the teaching of the pharisees were: 1) the acceptance of the Pentateuch, Prophets, and Writings as authoritative revelation, 2) belief in resurrection with rewards and punishments, 3) expectation of the Messiah who would set Israel free from Roman domination, 4) belief in angels, 5) the manifestation of an earthly paradise in which the righteous would dwell together with the resurrected righteous, and 6) stern attachment to the law in the form of a scrupulous observance of it.

As the sadducees are associated with the priesthood, so the scribes (also called lawyers) were associated with the pharisees. They were a special class of pharisees whose sole duty it was to study the law and interpret its meaning. They were the professional religious lawyers whereas the pharisees as a group were teachers of the law who also showed by their example how the law should be lived in daily life.

Of the four groups of leaders mentioned here the sadducees and the pharisees are the most prominent in the New Testament. In the first century B.C. they had been very hostile toward each other, even to the point of mutual persecution. It is likely that the authority of the Romans made it necessary for them to be more tolerant of each other. Even so, their hostility continued, as is evident from Paul's success in dividing them in their common opposition to him (Acts 23:6–10).

CHAPTER III
MATTHEW

Although Matthew was not the first of the gospels to be written, it has been placed first among them, thereby also becoming the first book of the New Testament. Three reasons may be given why Matthew should have priority both among the gospels and in the New Testament as a whole.

With the possible exception of Hebrews, Matthew provides a stronger connecting link between the Old and New Testaments than any other book in the New Testament. It was written for the Jews to show that Jesus is the fulfillment of Old Testament prophecy. Matthew contains many quotations from the Old Testament, using a large number of them to prove that in Jesus the Old Testament hopes of a messiah are realized. The very first verse of the book sets the theme for the whole: "The book of the genealogy of Jesus Christ, the son of David, the son of Abraham." Matthew therefore forms a remarkable point of connection and transition between the two testaments.

The second reason for Matthew's priority is the way in which it has been written. It is preeminently a *teaching* book. After a short introduction, the rest of the book is divided into definite sections that take turns in setting forth the *events* in the life of Jesus and the *teaching* of Jesus.

The third reason that accounts for Matthew's place in the New Testament is the fact that it balances its Jewish emphasis with a strong accent on the calling of the Gentiles. The wise men from the East greet Jesus at his birth, and the last words of the risen Lord are, "Go therefore and make disciples of all nations." Throughout the book the message of Christ for the nations is put forward again and again.

The canon of the New Testament and the order of the books in it developed in the course of the second, third, and fourth centuries. From the beginning the four gospels were given first place in the canon, and because of its character Matthew was given priority among the four.

AUTHOR

There is no indication in Matthew or in any other New Testament writing who authored the book called Matthew. It has, however, never been known by any other name. The Matthew in question is presumably the apostle (9:9; 10:3). He is also called Levi in Mark 2:14 and Luke 5:27–28. The earliest known association of Matthew with the authorship of the first gospel was made about 130 by a certain Papias, who is reported to have been the bishop of Hierapolis in Asia Minor. The church historian Eusebius (died *c* 340), in his *History of the Church*, quotes Papias to this effect: "Matthew compiled the *Sayings* in the Aramaic language, and everyone translated them as he could." What the "sayings" were that Papias had in mind has never been satisfactorily determined. The church fathers Irenaeus, Clement of Alexandria, Augustine, and Jerome considered Matthew the apostle to be the author. This view has remained the popular understanding to the present day. During the past century, however, New Testament studies have raised important questions about the authorship of Matthew.

A careful study of the first gospel indicates that it made large use of Mark. About ninety percent of the material in Mark appears in Matthew, sometimes with the very same wording. This is seen even more clearly in a comparison of the two gospels in Greek. But if it is true that Matthew borrowed from Mark, we must ask why a disciple of Jesus—who was one of the Twelve and therefore an eyewitness of his ministry--depended so heavily on the work of one who was not an apostle? The problem of authorship is further complicated by the fact that there is much material in Matthew that is also found in Luke but not in Mark. And, finally, there is considerable material in Matthew that is found neither in Luke nor in Mark.

The questions and problems arising from these data create the Synoptic Problem referred to in the first chapter. A more adequate discussion than is possible here is found in Chapter VII. With respect to the authorship of Matthew, however, we may summarize the findings of scholars as follows: Matthew the apostle originally composed in Aramaic a collection of teachings and possibly of deeds and events in Jesus' ministry, called the "Sayings" of Jesus. Subsequently a later writer or editor modified and expanded the "Sayings" to bring into being (in Greek) the present gospel. Meanwhile, whatever the manner in which the gospel received its final form, it continues to be known as "The Gospel According to Matthew."

Little is known about Matthew as a person, but that little is significant. He was a tax collector. Under the Roman occupation tax collectors were one of the most despised groups of people in Palestinian society. The expression "tax collectors and sinners" is found in Matthew 9:10, 11, Mark 2:15, 16, and in Luke 5:30. In Matthew 21:31 they are classified with prostitutes. There was good reason for this association. The Romans taxed heavily the countries that were under their control, dividing the provinces into districts and imposing a certain amount of tax on each district. The administration of the tax gathering in each district was usually in the hands of a Roman. He in turn hired local people to actually collect the taxes—the "tax collectors" mentioned in the gospels. Whatever they could collect above the amount required by the Roman district administrator went into their own pockets. The tax collectors therefore oppressed their own countrymen and were collaborators with the hated Roman conquerors. To this class Matthew belonged. He collected taxes in Galilee, presumably in the customs office on the main highway from Syria to Egypt. Along that road many travelers and great quantities of merchandise entered Palestine.

In selecting the Twelve, Jesus brought together a group of men who had little to commend themselves as founders of the church. James and John, the sons of anger, Thomas the doubter, Judas the traitor, Peter the tempestuous boaster, Simon the political radical, Matthew the tax collector—in these, with the exception of Judas, Jesus showed how in the kingdom of God the last can become first.

TIME AND PLACE OF WRITING

Since scholars are generally agreed that Mark was written between A.D. 65 and 70 and that Matthew was dependent upon him, the question arises, how much later was Matthew written? New Testament scholars differ greatly in estimating the date. Some place its writing in the seventies, others in the eighties, still others in the nineties and even early in the second century. Yet, the early popularity of Matthew in the church suggests that it was circulating widely at the end of the first century. All in all, the appearance of the gospel in its present form some time between 75 and 85 would seem to be as reasonable an estimate as any.

There is even less testimony to indicate where Matthew was written. General considerations point to Antioch in Syria. Matthew is a very Jewish book, but it also has an obvious and wide appeal for Gentiles. It is only because of this appeal that it could so soon have become the most used gospel in a predominantly Gentile church.

In Antioch, Jew and Gentile met. It was a large city. It was close to the Jewish homeland. It had a flourishing church. It had played a large role as Paul's missionary base. Antioch and Matthew were, therefore, entirely congenial to each other from the viewpoint of Matthew's writer. But this does not prove that Matthew was written in that city. All that can be said is that it could well have been written there.

READERS

The readers of a book are determined largely by the purpose for which it is written. In view of Matthew's strong interest in messianic fulfillment of the Old Testament, he doubtless considered that Jews would be his chief readers. These would be of two kinds: some Christian, the overwhelming majority traditionally Jewish. It is likely that he had both of these groups in mind. His writing would strengthen the faith of the former, and it would serve an evangelistic purpose in presenting the gospel to his Jewish countrymen as a whole. In showing Jesus to be the fulfillment of Old Testament hopes and prophecies, he would appeal to them to accept this fulfillment as God's great gift to Israel.

At the same time, it is clear that Matthew hoped for Gentile readers. His references to Gentiles, which sometimes give them priority over Israel in God's kingdom, and the general universal aspects of his gospel, indicate this. What in fact happened is that by the end of the first century Matthew had become the best-known gospel in the church, which was by that time mainly Gentile in character. Its Old Testament roots and its worldwide vision, its balance between event material and direct teaching material, the well-organized structure in which this balance is expressed, and its eminent suitability for teaching and public reading are the elements that brought this popularity about. In time, the Jewish readership that Matthew mainly had in mind virtually disappeared, and the Gentile readers whom he had only partly in mind became its main beneficiaries.

PURPOSE

Matthew was written to show that Jesus was the fulfillment of messianic prophecy. The word "messiah" comes from the Hebrew *mashiach*, which means "anointed one." In Israel, priests were anointed to qualify them for their office. On occasion prophets were anointed. Most especially, however, anointing was reserved to show the appointment of a man to be king. Among Israel's kings David was so much the greatest that he became a symbol, a type of the expected messiah. Matthew speaks of Jesus as "the son of David, the son of Abraham" (1:1). A nobler Jewish descent is not conceivable. Jesus was born in Bethlehem, the city of David. Blind men hailed him as the son of David (9:27; 20:30); his healing ministry led people to ask whether he might be the son of David (12:23); a Canaanite woman so regarded him (15:22); and crowds welcomed him on his return to Jerusalem from Galilee as the son of David who comes in the name of the Lord (21:9, 15; cf. also 1:16, 20; 2:2, 6). In addition, Jesus' enemies mocked him for his royal claims (27:29), and Pilate gave orders that the superscription "This is the king of the Jews" should be nailed on the cross above Jesus' head.

This Matthean witness to Jesus' messiahship stands in the midst of a broad context of Old Testament references. Jesus exercised his messianic authority by giving deeper and richer meaning to Old Testament teaching. The Sermon on the Mount is the supreme example of this. Apart from passing references to Old Testament words and phrases, Matthew adduces some sixty explicit quotations from the Old Testament, far more than are found in any other book of the New Testament. Of these about a fourth bear directly on Jesus' messianic mission. In order of their appearance they are: 2:6 (Micah 5:2); 2:15 (Hosea 11:1); 3:3 (Isa. 40:3); 4:15 (Isa. 9:1, 2); 8:17 (Isa. 53:4); 11:10 (Mal. 3:1); 12:18–21 (Isa. 41:9; 42:1–4); 12:40 (Jonah 1:2); 21:5 (Isa. 62:11; Zech. 9:9); 21:42 (Ps. 118:22, 23); 23:39 (Ps. 118:26); 26:31 (Zech. 13:7); 26:64 (Dan. 7:13); 27:46 (Ps. 22:1).

So basic was this messianic ministry that Jesus received the name Christ, from the Greek *christos*, also meaning "anointed one." This was the heart of Peter's declaration, "You are the Christ, the Son of the living God" (16:16). It was because he was to discharge this saving role in the life of Israel and humanity that he was at his birth given the personal name Jesus, which means "savior" (1:21).

Messianic prophecy included several basic elements in its message. The messiah would be a Jew. He would be completely identified with the Jewish people. He would bless them with spiritual renewal—a renewal that would look beyond Israel and make it the instrument for the salvation of the world. Abraham, the father of Israel, had been called in order that through him all the families of the earth might be blessed. The theme of universal outreach of the gospel, therefore, is an essential part of the fulfillment of Old Testament prophecy, which climaxes in the Great Commission (28:18–20).

Matthew unfolds its message in two major stages. The first, that of the preaching of the kingdom, extends from 4:12 to 16:20. In 4:17 the theme for this section is given with the proclamation: "From that time Jesus began to preach, saying, 'Repent, for the kingdom of heaven is at hand.' " The second stage extends from 16:21 to the end of the book. Its theme is found in the first verse of this section: "From that time Jesus began to show his disciples that he must go to Jerusalem and suffer many things from the elders and chief priests and scribes and be killed and on the third day be raised." This does not mean, however, that Matthew is controlled by two unrelated themes, one about the kingdom, the other about Jesus' suffering. Rather, the kingdom that Jesus preached is realized through the suffering and death that he endured.

STRUCTURE

There is no book in the New Testament that has been more skillfully and simply arranged than Matthew. It opens with a brief introductory section (1:1–2:23), followed by the great central portion of the book describing the ministry of Jesus (chs. 3–25). This section consists of ten regularly interchanging historical and instructional sections. We shall call them simply events and teaching sections. The book then closes with an account of Jesus' passion, death, and resurrection (chs. 26–28). The structure of Matthew is as follows:

INTRODUCTION
1:1–2:23
GENEALOGY AND BIRTH OF JESUS,
VISIT OF THE WISE MEN,
HOSTILITY OF HEROD

MINISTRY
3:1–25:46

EVENTS	TEACHING
3:1–4:25	
Preaching of John the Baptist, temptation of Jesus, withdrawal to Galilee, beginning of preaching, call of the first disciples, healing	
	5, 6, 7
	Sermon on the Mount

(EVENTS)   (TEACHING)
8:1–9:34
Works of Jesus

                                                    9:35–10:42
                                                    Work for the disciples

11, 12
John the Baptist's question,
Rebuke of the three cities,
Controversy

                                                    13
                                                    Parables of the Kingdom

14–17
Death of John the Baptist,
miracles, Peter's confession,
suffering foretold, transfiguration,
fishing for tax money

                                                    18
                                                    Teaching on humility

19–23
Departure from Galilee,
controversy, miracles, various
teachings. Suffering again foretold.
Entry into Jerusalem. Rebuke of
the scribes and Pharisees

                                    24, 25
                                    Prophecies concerning the End-time

PASSION AND RESURRECTION
26, 27, 28
Last Supper, betrayal, trial, crucifixion,
resurrection, the great commission.

The following features should be noted about the ten sections
in general:

1. Each teaching section is skillfully related to the preceding
events section by a connecting sentence. As an example we may
consider the transition from the events section of chapters 14–17 to
the teaching section of chapter 18, and then the transition to the
next events section, which begins with chapter 19. Chapter 18 begins with a reference to the last words of the preceding events section in the words, "At that time. . . ." This opens the way for the
discourse. Then in 19:1 "Now when Jesus had finished these sayings
. . ." marks the change-over to the events section.

2. Events section 8:1–9:34 shows three groups of miracles:

8:1–17, 8:23–9:8, and 9:18–34. In the events section 14:1–17:27 there are again three groups of miracles: 14:13–26, 15:21–39, and 17:1–27. In the reading it should be remembered that Matthew was not written in chapters. Therefore no attention should be paid to the chapter divisions. In each section the various groups of miracles are separated by passages that are mainly used for teaching purposes. The parables in the teaching section of chapter 13 are seven in number, the chief symbolic number in Scripture.

3. Four of the five teaching sections deal with Jesus' *private* ministry to his disciples. Only the Sermon on the Mount is entirely public. The parables given in chapter 13 were partly spoken in public, partly in private. It should be observed, however, that *explanations* of parables are given only to the disciples. The events sections, on the other hand, deal mainly with the public words and actions of Jesus. There are, though, substantial passages in them that concern Jesus' relation to his disciples, such as 4:18–22; 14:22–33; 16:5–28; 19:25–30.

4. The Sermon on the Mount (chapters 5–7) is a highly distinctive part not only of Matthew, but of the Bible as a whole. No segment of Scripture moves at a higher level of moral and religious power. It must be noted that the Sermon has a definite structure. The reading of it will be even more profitable when this structure is understood and kept in mind.

In his little book *Design For Life*, A. M. Hunter sets forth the pattern of the Sermon. We follow here the main lines of his analysis.

a) The first part of Jesus' design for life in the kingdom is a description of the character of that life. It is one of blessedness. It is set forth in the well-known opening beatitudes (from *beatus*, the Latin word for blessed) (5:1–12). The effect of such a life is to enrich its surroundings with salt and light (5:13–16).

b) This life of blessedness is related to the life the Jews had lived under the law, but at the same time it supersedes it. Jesus came not to destroy the law but to fulfill it (5:17–20). Six weighty paragraphs begin with, "You have heard that it was said . . . but I say to you . . ." (5:41–48). Through Christ the law reaches its fulfillment in the kingdom.

c) A shorter section (6:1–18) is concerned with worship. It contrasts the prevailing practice with spiritual requirements. Jesus touches here on giving, prayer, and fasting.

d) The fourth and last section (6:19–7:23) sets forth the cultivation and practice of life in the kingdom. It does so in two ways. The first (6:19–34) is wholly concerned with the personal internal growth of the spiritual life. The neighbor does not enter into it. The man-to-God and the man-to-self relationships receive the attention here. The second (7:1–23), however, deals with spiritual growth by way of interaction with others.

e) The conclusion of the Sermon (7:24–28) is the well-known parable of the two houses, the one built on sand, the other on rock.

CHARACTERISTICS

When we speak of "characteristics" in discussing the gospels in this book, we have in mind emphases and viewpoints that are distinctive of the particular gospel in question. We have already noted some. Below, the more outstanding characteristics of Matthew are set forth, including some elaborations on those already mentioned.

1. CONTINUITY BETWEEN THE TESTAMENTS

It is especially Matthew, we have noted, which establishes continuity between the Old and the New Testaments. It does this chiefly by quoting frequently from the Old Testament. In doing so, it often introduces the quotation with a particular expression made in one form or another. The most common form is "that it might be fulfilled . . . ," examples of which are found in 1:22, 23; 2:15; 2:17; 2:23; 3:3; 4:14–16; 8:17; 12:17–21; 13:35; 21:4, 5; 26:56.

2. PARTICULARISM AND UNIVERSALISM

Two great emphases run parallel to each other throughout the book. They are the special place of Israel in God's plan of salvation, and the inclusion of the Gentiles in that plan. These emphases are often referred to as *Israel's particularism* and *Gentile universalism*. The genealogy with which Matthew begins his gospel shows Jesus to be a true son of Israel. He is a descendant of Abraham the father of the nation, and of David the great king. He has been sent only to the lost sheep of the house of Israel (15:24), and it is to them that he sends out his disciples to preach and to heal. His style of life, his religious life, his familiar social environment, and his most intimate fellowships are all distinctively Jewish.

With this particularism, however, there is inseparably bound up a universal message. Indeed, the universalism is, as it were, rooted in the particularism. For example, in the very genealogy that establishes Jesus' Jewishness, four women are listed who were not Jewish: Tamar (1:3), Rahab and Ruth (vs. 5), and Bathsheba, the wife of Uriah, the mother of Solomon (vs. 6). It should also be noted that apart from Mary these women are the only ones listed in the genealogy. In addition, the wise men from the East were Gentiles, and Egypt, the place of refuge for the holy family, was Gentile.

Throughout the book there are references to Gentiles: a Canaanite woman is praised for her faith (8:5–13), as is also a Roman officer (15:22–28); Jesus will be a blessing to the Gentiles (12:18–21), and many shall come from east and west to enter the kingdom (8:11, 12). Many similar passages can be found, among which the most notable is the Great Commission (28:18–20).

3. DISCONTINUITY BETWEEN THE TESTAMENTS

As universalism stands alongside of particularism, so *discontinuity* between the old and the new covenants stands alongside of the *continuity* between them. Matthew emphasizes both aspects strongly. The new situation that Jesus brings into being is of one piece with the old out of which it comes, and yet it is wholly distinct from it. "You have heard that it was said to men of old. . . . But I say to you . . ." is found no less than six times in the Sermon on the Mount (5:21–44). Jesus also goes beyond Jewish law and custom to establish a morality that has a new spiritual depth (9:10–13; 9:14–17; 12:1–8; 15:1–20; 22:23–33). The law of the Old Testament is not put away; it is given a richer meaning. Thus, the gospel is rooted in the life and history of Israel, and its fruit is for all the world.

4. KINGDOM OF HEAVEN

A marked feature of Matthew is its use of the term "the kingdom of heaven." It has the same meaning as "the kingdom of God," the expression used in the other gospels and throughout the New Testament. The reason for Matthew's usage is probably the Jews' reluctance to use the name of God. In the postexilic period the Jews refrained from using the proper name of God, *Yahweh*, and in its place used *Adonai*, which means "Lord." It is this reverence that Matthew honors in using the expression "kingdom of heaven."

5. THE CHURCH GOSPEL

Matthew is often referred to as "the church gospel." More than any of the other gospels it appears to have been written with the practical needs of the church in mind. It is the only gospel that uses the word "church" (16:18; 18:17). It records the Great Commission (28:18–20) as the law of the church's life for the worldwide expansion of the faith. It is the only gospel that speaks of baptism in the name of the triune God, which has, since early times, been the means of entry into the church. In the absence of printed gospels Matthew was doubtless much used in public reading as part of the worship of the church. Teachers and evangelists could also use it effectively as a means of catechesis, that is, instruction of seekers and converts in the Christian faith. It lays down rules for resolving difficulties between members of the church (18:15–18), and the binding character of decisions of the church in these matters. The worship of the church as well as its evangelistic witness are sanctified and made effective by the presence of Christ (18:20; 28:20).

6. THE TEACHING GOSPEL

As Matthew may be called "the church gospel," so it may with equal right be called "the teaching gospel." Its structure—which we have noted in some detail—lends itself to this purpose. Eight of its chapters are definitely oral teaching chapters. They are: a) the Sermon on the Mount (chs. 5–7), b) instructions for evangelism given to the Twelve (ch. 10), c) teaching by parables (ch. 13), d) instructions about greatness and forgiveness in the kingdom of heaven (ch. 18), and e) discourse on the End-time (chs. 24, 25). It may not be forgotten, however, that Jesus taught by deeds as well as by words. His humility in willingness to undergo baptism (ch. 3), his resistance of temptation (ch. 4), his healing ministry (notably in ch. 8 and 9), his rebuke of religion that is not from the heart, his fearlessness in the face of opposition, especially from the pharisees, his patience, his kindness, his constancy in prayer, his example of meekness in suffering to the point of death—and all of these foreshadowed in the humbleness of his birth in a stable—are no less a part of his ministry than is his oral teaching. Indeed, it may be said that his example of the obedient life constitutes the seal of truth and sincerity on his oral instruction. The example of his holy life makes his oral teaching convincing.

There are, finally, literary and theological characteristics of Matthew that can be more appropriately discussed in connection with the Synoptic Problem, and will therefore be discussed in Chapter VII.

CHAPTER IV

MARK

According to most New Testament scholars, Mark was the first of the four gospels to be written, which gives the book a significance that the others cannot claim. That is, it was John Mark who created the literary form of writing known as "a gospel." It was he who first made use of the reportorial narrative form of writing to set forth the meaning of the good news about Jesus Christ. In doing so, Mark set the pattern for the other gospels. The extensive differences that exist between Mark and the other gospels do not change the fact that it is Mark who opened the way for Matthew, Luke, and probably John to be written. And it is evident that nearly the whole of Mark is found in Matthew and fifty percent in Luke. It is, therefore, a fundamentally important book for our study.

AUTHOR

The writer of the second gospel is generally considered to be John Mark, an assistant of three eminent leaders of the earliest church, namely, Peter, Paul, and Barnabas. The New Testament contains several references to him. One of these (Acts 13:13) reports that Mark left Paul and Barnabas on Paul's first missionary journey and returned to Jerusalem. The ill feeling that this caused in Paul later led to a break between him and Barnabas (Acts 15:36–41). The "sharp contention" between these two Christian leaders suggests that Mark had a defense for his action, but we do not know what it was.

This unpleasant incident has been much remembered in the church, which tends to obscure the fact that a reconciliation later took place between Paul and Mark, and that Mark became Paul's trusted assistant (Col. 4:10; II Tim. 4:11; Philemon 24). His close relationship to Peter (I Peter 5:13) contributed much in preparing him for the writing of the gospel account. Since it is the major source for Matthew and Luke, and because an early tradition holds that Mark became the first bishop of the church in Alexandria, it will be useful to indicate what is known of Mark as a person.

Our first acquaintance with him comes sometime between A.D. 41 and 44, when Herod Agrippa reigned over Judea. During this time Peter was arrested, imprisoned, and miraculously freed (Acts 12). We are told that upon gaining his freedom he went to the home of Mary "the mother of John whose other name was Mark," where a number of believers were praying for him. Mark was, therefore, a member of a Christian family in Jerusalem. (Mark's father may not have been a Christian or may have died before the events recorded in Acts 12 occurred, which could account for identifying the family by the mother rather than by the father.) Peter must have been well acquainted with their home since he sought refuge there when he escaped. Thus, it is reasonable to suppose that early on Mark and Peter knew each other. Indeed, Peter's reference to Mark as "my son" (I Pet. 5:13) may indicate that Mark was his spiritual child, that is, that he had brought Mark to the faith.

In due course John Mark became an assistant to Paul and Barnabas on Paul's first missionary journey. Later he accompanied Barnabas (Acts 15:39). The difficulty with Paul was overcome in time, as we have noted. Peter's greeting at the end of his first epistle not only indicates that Mark was with him at that time but also that the place was probably Rome. The expression "she that is in Babylon" is in all likelihood a code reference to the church in Rome (cf. Rev. 17:5; 18:2). Mark therefore had intimate knowledge of the two foremost apostles, and he was an associate of Barnabas who was an apostle in a looser sense of the word (Acts 14:14). Through his connection with Paul and Peter, Mark was doubtless also well acquainted with the life of the church in the city of Rome.

There is no direct evidence in the gospel that Mark is its author. A strong tradition, however, ascribes the writing of it to him. The oldest witness to that effect is Papias, bishop of Hierapolis in Asia Minor, whom we met in the preceding chapter. Quoting a certain elder John of Ephesus, Papias wrote:

> This, too, the presbyter [i.e., the elder John] used to say: "Mark, who had been Peter's interpreter, wrote down carefully, but not in order, all that he remembered of the Lord's sayings and doings. For he had not heard the Lord or been one of his followers, but later, as I said, one of Peter's. Peter used to adapt his teaching to the occasion, without making a systematic arrangement of the Lord's sayings, so that Mark was quite justified in writing down some things just as he remembered them. For he had one purpose only—to leave out nothing that he had heard, and to make no misstatement about it" (Eusebius, *History of the Church from Christ to Constantine*, III, 39).

That John Mark was the author of the gospel according to Mark was the common testimony of such leading figures in the early church as Irenaeus, Clement of Alexandria, Origen, and Jerome as well as of Papias. It is also the belief of most modern scholars. There are some, however, who call Mark's authorship into question. They advance the consideration that Mark (Latin: Marcus) was a very common name in the Roman empire. Some Christian in Rome by that name who was well acquainted with Peter may, they feel, have been the author. An additional argument is that some inexact references to Palestine in the gospel would be more understandable if the writer were not a Palestinian which Mark doubtless was. These considerations have not, however, shaken the prevailing view that the John Mark we meet in the Acts of the Apostles is the author of the gospel according to Mark.

READERS

There is reason to believe that Mark was written with Gentile readers strongly in mind. Little in Mark corresponds to Matthew's large effort to relate Jesus and his work to the Old Testament as a fulfillment of it. Mark is based squarely on the Old Testament and has many references to it, but it does not use them as obviously or in such a Jewish way as Matthew does. In a number of passages that have the same event or teaching in mind, Matthew adds distinctively Jewish material that is absent in Mark. For example, about the troubles in the last days Mark reads, "Pray that it may not happen in winter" (13:18). Matthew adds the touch, "or on a sabbath" (24:20). Both report Jesus' dialogue with the Syro-phoenician woman, but in his account Matthew quotes Jesus as saying, "I was sent only to the lost sheep of the house of Israel" (15:24); Mark does not record this statement (7:24–30). In Mark 6:7–11 the Twelve are simply sent out by Jesus to teach and to heal; in Matthew's account (10:5, 6) Jesus instructs his disciples not to go to the Gentiles or to the Samaritans, but only to the lost sheep of the house of Israel. Thus, Mark's nonreference to Jewish backgrounds in such contexts may well indicate that he had a Gentile readership in mind.

At the same time, however, the entire setting of Mark is Palestinian. The Jewish context is everywhere present and sometimes the writer makes plain the Jewish contexts that the non-Jewish reader might otherwise not understand, as in 7:3, 4; 15:42; 14:12. But this does not obscure the universal intent of the gospel. It would be hard to imagine a more universal introduction for a gospel than that recorded in the opening verse of the book, "The beginning of the gospel of Jesus Christ, the Son of God." But this is again immediately followed by a quotation from the Old Testament. It is this combination of universal and Jewish emphases that make Mark an ideal gospel for a community that was predominantly Gentile but with a substantial Jewish element in it. The church in Rome was precisely such a congregation.

Matthew, as we have seen, has a marked Gentile reference in his gospel alongside his Jewish emphasis. In this repect Mark and Matthew share common ground. Matthew, however, reenforced the Jewish background and concern of his gospel by strong and repeated demonstrations of Old Testament fulfillment in Christ. This Mark did not do. Herein lies one of the major differences between Matthew and Mark.

TIME AND PLACE OF WRITING

Mark does not indicate when the book was written. What we do know is that it was written before Matthew and Luke were. This will be noted at some length in our discussion of the Synoptic Problem. There is, however, considerable external evidence for the approximate date of writing. Irenaeus, writing about A.D. 200, said that Mark wrote his gospel after Peter's death. On the other hand, Clement of Alexandria, who wrote some twenty-five years earlier, reported that it was written during Peter's lifetime. About 130, Papias, the earliest witness of all, suggests in the words "from memory" that Mark wrote after Peter's death.

It is clear that the evidence immediately relates Mark's writing to Peter, whether before or after his death. According to a long held tradition Peter was executed under Nero about 64. When we combine these data with the early origin of Mark as compared with Matthew and Luke, the approximate time of writing between 65 and 70 would seem to be a wholly reasonable supposition.

From early times there has been a strong tradition that Mark wrote the gospel in Rome. The reason for this is doubtless his close association with Peter in the last days of Peter's life. I Peter 5:13 places Peter in Rome and tradition makes him a martyr in that city in the Neronian persecution. Presumably Mark was in Rome at the time. Papias' testimony establishes, as we have seen, a strong connection between Peter and Mark. Clement of Alexandria and Irenaeus indicate that Mark was written in Rome or in Italy. Moreover, Mark was not as popular a gospel in the early church as were the other three. Its survival and acceptance as a canonical book may well be due to the support which it received from the influential Roman church.

PURPOSE

Mark's purpose, like Matthew's (though less directly), is to show that Jesus is the Messiah.* Since the community for which he wrote was in large part Gentile, Mark introduced Jesus to his readers as "the Son of God" (1:1), as Gentile readers would understand this better than the Hebrew idea of messiah. At the same time, the title "Son of God" was wholly agreeable to Jewish messianic thinking. Having done so, then, he develops his account in such a way that the two ideas flow into one. (It may be questioned whether the centurion in 15:39 had in mind the biblical conception of Son of God. He said "a son of God," not "the Son of God.") While using Old Testament material, Mark's chief evidence for Jesus' messianic character is not fulfilled prophecy as in Matthew, but Jesus, Jesus himself.

Mark set forth Jesus in his claims, Jesus in his mighty works, Jesus in his preaching and teaching, Jesus in his suffering, Jesus in his death and resurrection. But there is more than this. He set forth the response of men to Jesus and his work. For example, he reports the overwhelming public reaction to Jesus' healing and teaching ministry. It is Mark—and Mark alone—who records this simple but unsurpassed tribute to Jesus' preaching and teaching: "And the common people heard him gladly" (12:37). Already in the first part of chapter 2 we see the confidence of the ordinary people in Jesus' ability to heal; we note the hostile reaction of the Jewish religious leadership, and the praise of the people, ". . . they were all amazed and glorified God, saying, 'We never saw anything like this' " (2:12). He records, several times, the recognition and fear of Christ on the part of the demons.

These elements are certainly not lacking in Matthew. But in Mark they stand out more prominently as main pillars supporting his presentation of Jesus.

The message that Jesus spoke was understandable to both Jews and Gentiles. Mark sets it forth in a few words in 1:15—"The time is fulfilled and the kingdom of God is at hand; repent and believe in the gospel." A Jewish reader would understand this to mean: The

*For the meaning of "messiah" see the section on Purpose in the preceding chapter.

promise of God given to the fathers that he would visit his people has been realized; the rule of God is about to begin. A Gentile reading the same words would understand: The God who made all things is about to establish his kingly rule among men. To both, Mark says: Enter the kingdom by repenting of your sins and believing in the good news that Jesus proclaimed. The gospel according to Mark is a book for Jews looking for their Messiah; it is a book for Gentiles seeking the way to God.

CHARACTERISTICS

The contents of Mark are basic elements in the gospels of Matthew and Luke. This circumstance largely accounts for the similarity of the three gospels. In trying to understand the distinctiveness of Mark, therefore, it will be necessary to note the more important characteristic features of this gospel.

1. TITLE

Mark is the only gospel that has a title in the text. It is, "the beginning of the gospel of Jesus Christ, the Son of God" (1:1). That is to say, it proposes to describe how the *euangelion*—the gospel, the good news about Jesus Christ—came into being. In doing so, of course, it describes the good news itself. It is likely that Mark, in using the word *euangelion* (Greek for "good news"), provided the title which the church later applied to all four accounts of the ministry of Jesus now known as gospels.*

2. LIMTED INTRODUCTION

Mark required only thirteen verses to bring his account to the beginning of Jesus' ministry. Eight of these are given to an introductory paragraph about John the Baptist, three to Jesus' baptism, and two to the temptation in the wilderness. After that, from 1:14 on, he reports Jesus' ministry. Mark therefore contains no account of Jesus' birth. It also contains no report about Jesus before his baptism. He apparently did not consider such knowledge essential for understanding the message of the gospel.**

3. NON-USE OF "LORD"

The almost complete absence of the word "Lord" as a title of Jesus is distinctive of Mark. The Greek word for lord, *kurios*, means "master" or "owner." In direct address it means "sir." Both Matthew and Luke make frequent use of this word as a title for Jesus. They refer to him directly as Lord: "When the Lord saw her he had compassion on her" (Luke 7:13); they record the disciples

*For the meaning of "gospel" cf. Chapter 1.
**This would also appear to be the case with John.

addressing him as such: "Lord, even the demons are subject to us" (Luke 10:17); and in them Jesus refers to himself as Lord: "Not everyone who says to me, Lord, Lord, shall enter into the kingdom of heaven" (Matt. 7:21). Mark, on the other hand, makes almost no use of the title in referring to Jesus. In 2:28 where the King James Version has "Lord," the Revised Standard Version more properly has "lord," that is, master" (as also in the New English Bible). In 11:3 the R.S.V. translates *kurios* as "master," but in terms of Mark's usage the rendering "lord" would have been quite appropriate.

The difference between Mark on the one hand and Matthew and Luke on the other is therefore significant. Matthew and Luke write about Jesus' ministry from the postresurrection point of view. That is, before the resurrection the disciples had a very imperfect understanding of Jesus' character and purpose. After the resurrection, however, they saw him as the Son of God, the Prince of glory, the Savior of men. The church's favorite postresurrection designation of Jesus was "Lord." Matthew and Luke carry this postresurrection designation back into the time before the resurrection, but Mark does this hardly at all. He therefore places a stronger emphasis on Jesus' preresurrection humanity than do Matthew and Luke. His favorite title for Jesus is Teacher.

4. HUMAN CHARACTER

Mark's infrequent use of *kurios* in referring to Jesus helps to clarify another marked feature of the gospel. He permitted himself to make franker and more human statements about Jesus than either of the other two Synoptists considered proper. This is especially evident from the way in which Matthew and Luke modify material that they take over from Mark.

a) Concerning the storm on the Sea of Galilee during which Jesus slept in a boat, Mark writes about the disciples: "and they woke him and said, 'Teacher, do you not care if we perish'?" (4:38). Luke, apparently unwilling to suggest that Jesus might be indifferent to the welfare of his disciples, writes, "Master, master, we are perishing!" (8:24), indicating only the fear of the disciples. Similarly Matthew, "Save, Lord, we are perishing!" (8:25). (Matthew characteristically translates *kurios* as "Lord." The Greek word in Luke is *epistata*, "master." Mark has neither; he uses *didaskalos*, "teacher.")

b) In 6:5 Mark writes, "And he could do no mighty works there" because of the unbelief of his fellow townsmen. Matthew, writing about the same incident, says, "And he did not do many mighty works there" (13:58). Mark's "could do no" becomes "did not do" in Matthew, and "no mighty works" becomes "(not) many mighty works." Matthew preserves in a very literal way Jesus' ability to perform miracles in the face of men's unbelief.

c) Mark quotes a certain man coming to Jesus as saying to him, "Good Teacher, what must I do to inherit eternal life?" To this Jesus replied, "Why do you call me good? No one is good but God alone" (10:17). Matthew writes, "Teacher, what good deed must I do to have eternal life?" To which Jesus replied, "Why do you ask me about what is good? One there is who is good" (19:17). By making the adjective "good" apply to "deed" and "what" instead of to "Teacher" and "me," Matthew protects Jesus against the thought that he might not be sinless (which of course Mark did not intend).

d) In connection with point (c) above, it is interesting to notice that Luke in distinction from Matthew takes Mark over literally here. However, Luke as well as Matthew omits Mark's interesting observation in 10:21, "And Jesus looking upon him, loved him."

5. JESUS' DIVINE SONSHIP

The fact that Mark emphasized Jesus' humanity does not mean that he underestimated his character as Son of God. He set the two next to each other without trying to take anything from either and also without trying to harmonize them or explain them. The gospel opens with "The beginning of the gospel of Jesus Christ the Son of God." The heavenly Father himself witnesses to Christ's sonship twice (1:11; 9:7), and even the demons recognize him as such (1:24; 3:11; 5:7). In 12:7, 37 Jesus' divine sonship is implied. In 13:32 and 14:61, 62 Jesus himself clearly affirms it. He even forgives sins (2:5–12). Alongside of these passages stands also the witness of Jesus' words and claims and attitudes, all of which breathe authority and inspire awe of his person. Mark as well as Matthew and Luke shows the postresurrection view of Jesus in describing his preresurrection life. But he did not permit this to obscure the intense humanity that characterized our Lord in his earthly life.

6. PLACE OF PASSION NARRATIVE

In all the gospels the suffering, death, and resurrection of Jesus constitute both a very extensive and the climactic part of the books. The large proportion of Mark's gospel (from 10:32 to 15:47) is devoted to the last weeks of Jesus' life, and doubtless set the pattern for the other gospels.

7. GOSPEL OF ACTION

Mark emphasizes action. It therefore gives less attention to teaching. There is indeed a great deal of teaching in Mark, but it is a teaching by example, by deeds of love and mercy. In the course

of this teaching by deed Jesus speaks again and again, but his words
are more remarks than speeches, usually less than five verses. Sometimes there is no explanation of his actions at all. Rather, there is
constant movement. Mark's favorite way of designating this movement is by means of the word "immediately," used some forty times
in his gospel. A striking example is found in 1:29–31:

> And immediately he left the synagogue, and entered into the house of
> Simon and Andrew, with James and John. Now Simon's mother-in-
> law lay sick with a fever. And immediately they told him of her. . . .

8. MANNER OF TEACHING

While teaching in the form of discourse does not stand on
the foreground in Mark, Jesus' teaching by word of mouth is by no
means absent from the book. Chapter 4 is almost entirely given to
teaching by parables. Chapter 13 is in its entirety an eschatological
discourse. There are in other chapters sections of eight, eleven,
twelve, and seventeen verses. More significant are the many references in the book to teaching that has not been reported. For example, Jesus came into Galilee preaching and teaching the good
tidings of the kingdom of God (1:14). On the Sabbath he entered
into the synagogue and taught (1:22). He taught multitudes by the
sea (2:13; 4:1). The common people heard him gladly, (12:37). At
the transfiguration a heavenly voice said, "This is my beloved Son,
listen to him" (9:7). These references show that for Mark also Jesus'
preaching and teaching occupied a very large place in his ministry,
even though its content is not disclosed.

9. SHORT GOSPEL

With sixteen chapters, Mark is by far the shortest of the
gospels. This must, however, be correctly understood. It does not
report anything about Jesus' life before his ministry began. It includes relatively little discourse material. It is mainly these circumstances that account for the brevity of Mark.

10. ENDING OF GOSPEL

The oldest and most authoritative manuscripts of Mark end
at 16:8. Some scholars believe that that is where Mark ended his
gospel. There are strong arguments against this view, however. In
Mark's resurrection account we do not actually meet the risen Jesus;
there is only an angelic report of his resurrection. This seems strange.
There is also no command to the disciples to preach the gospel as
we find in Matthew, Luke, and John. The merits of verses 9–20 as
we have them in a footnote in the R.S.V. are debatable. The basic
reason for their exclusion from the text, however, is their absence
from the two most authoritative ancient manuscripts, Sinaiticus and

Vaticanus. It is significant that some manuscripts have a shorter conclusion, appended after verse 8, which reads, "But they reported briefly to Peter and those with him all that they had been told. And after this, Jesus himself sent out by means of them, from east to west, the sacred and imperishable proclamation of salvation." This would appear to indicate that some at least in the early church did not feel comfortable either with the absence of a more appropriate ending or with verses 9–20. It seems reasonable therefore to assume that the original of the last part of chapter 16 was lost at an early date or, due to circumstances not known to us, was never written.

STRUCTURE

Mark has been written in a manner altogether different from the carefully structured Matthew. The regular rotation of event and discourse sections is wholly absent from Mark. We find rather a continuous account of events interrupted at two points by discourse sections of one chapter each, chapter 4 on parables and chapter 13 on eschatology. Chapter 13 may be viewed as separating Jesus' public ministry in Judea (chs. 10, 11, 12) from the account of his passion, death, and resurrection (chs. 14, 15, 16). Chapter 4 on the parables does not appear to make a similar division. Rather, the material that precedes and follows it is substantially of the same narrative character. Mark is therefore best described as a long events narrative broken by two discourses.

It is possible, however, to discover a *geographical* division in Mark. The division that can be made on this basis consists of a five-point arrangement:

    I. Judea: Jesus' Preparation for his Ministry (1:1–13)
   II. Galilee and Environs (1:14–9:50)
      A. Preaching, Teaching and Healing (1:14–8:26)
      B. Emphasis on Impending Suffering (8:27–9:50)
  III. Return from Galilee to Judea (10:1–52)
  IV. Judea and Jerusalem (11:1–13:37)
      A. Controversy (11:1–12:44)
      B. Eschatological Discourse (13:1–37)
   V. Jerusalem: Last Supper to Resurrection (14:1–16:8
     [9–20])

This geographical outline is characteristic of all the Synoptics. Because of additional material incorporated in Matthew and Luke, the outline comes to its clearest expression in Mark.

CHAPTER V
LUKE

The gospel of Luke has from the beginning had its own distinctive place both in the canon of the New Testament and in the affection of the church. It does not have the careful structure of Matthew. It lacks the depth of John. It uses Mark extensively and draws in much material from sources outside of Mark. Nevertheless, in many ways it is the most attractive of the gospels. It begins with the joyous announcements of the birth of Jesus. It concludes with a wonderfully moving account of Jesus' resurrection appearance to two disciples on the road to Emmaus. In between lie twenty-one chapters of fascinating description of the ministry of Jesus. It is by common consent the most literary of the gospels, and in the judgment of scholars uses the purest Greek. Moreover, Luke has the unusual distinction of having a companion book in the Acts of the Apostles. The two books are really one continuous account: the one presenting the work of Christ in the flesh, the other its continuation in the life of the church through the Holy Spirit. And as Mark lent authority to his gospel by his association with Peter, so Luke lends authority to his by his association with Paul.

AUTHOR

The gospel of Luke, like those of Matthew and Mark, does not state who its author is. Acts also gives no specific indication of authorship by name. However, both books do state very clearly for whom they were written, namely, a certain friend or acquaintance of the author named Theophilus. The introductory words to Theophilus in Luke 1:1–4 make some significant statements about the book's author. We are told that he was not an eyewitness of the events that he recorded; on the contrary, his report depends on the accounts of those who were eyewitnesses. These accounts were apparently not wholly satisfactory to the author of our gospel. He leaves the impression that they were wanting in some respects, but in which respects is not indicated. He had therefore examined all things "closely," and that not briefly but "for some time past." Having completed his inquiries and investigations, he is now ready to write "an orderly account" with the purpose that Theophilus may "know the truth" about Jesus concerning whose life and work he had apparently been informed earlier.

The tradition that Luke, "the beloved physician" (Col. 4:14), is the author of both the gospel and Acts goes back to the first half of the second century. Authorities as widely distant from each other as Tertullian in North Africa, Irenaeus in Gaul, Origen in Alexandria, and Marcion in Asia Minor refer to Luke as the author. These data are further strengthened by the fact that Luke's authorship was at no time called into question in the early church.

However strong the tradition of Lukan authorship may be, the most important evidence for it comes not from tradition, nor from the gospel, but from Acts. There are two matters about which there can be no doubt. One is that both Luke and Acts were written for or dedicated to the same person, Theophilus. The other is that both books were written by the same author. This is clear from Luke 1:1–4 and Acts 1:1. Thus, we have a common dedication to a person whose name we know, and a common authorship by a person whose name we do not know. The question we must try to answer is: Who is the author of these two books?

The extent of evidence that we have for Lukan authorship is limited, but what we do have is significant. It may be summarized as follows: As a whole, Acts is written in the third person. Presumably the account is based on carefully collected data, as in the case of the gospel. This data was then written up in narrative form. The action that the narrator describes took place, so far as our knowledge goes, quite apart from him. There are four substantial sections, however, in which the narrator identifies himself with Paul and his companions, speaking in terms of we, us, or our. These are the much discussed "we-sections," which range in length from eight to sixty verses and are found in 16:10–17; 20:5–21:18; 27:1–28:16. In the long passage 20:16–38 there is no "we" reference, but it was quite clearly a part of the author's experience (cf. 21:1). All of these references are in the second part of Acts, it should be noted, in which the Gentile mission is the central subject and Paul the central figure.

Is it possible to determine who wrote the we-sections? If it is, we would have a strong pointer to the author of both Luke and Acts. A firm identification does not appear to be possible. What can be said is that certain significant circumstances support the tradition that Luke wrote them. These circumstances are the following:

1. Luke is mentioned in the text of the New Testament in three of Paul's letters:

Col. 4:14:   Luke the beloved physician and Demas greet
                    you . . .
Philemon 23, 24: Epaphras, my fellow prisoner in Christ Jesus,
                    sends greetings to you, and so do Mark,
                    Aristarchus, Demas, and Luke, my fellow
                    workers . . .
II Tim. 4:11:   Luke alone is with me . . .

2. All three of the above letters were written in prison, and Luke was present with Paul at the writing of each one of them. The New Testament records only one imprisonment of Paul, namely, that which was occasioned by his arrest in Jerusalem and subsequent events leading to a two-year, semi-imprisonment in Rome (28:30). It is probable that Paul was released from this imprisonment but was again arrested two years later, this second imprisonment ending by his execution under Nero about A.D. 64.

3. It was during the Roman imprisonment, in all probability, that Colossians and Philemon were written (Col. 4:10, 18; Philemon 1, 9, 10, 23. It is likely that Paul's "Luke alone is with me" (II Tim. 4:11), was written during his second imprisonment.

4. Besides Luke, Paul had three other traveling companions: Timothy, Silas, and Titus. Timothy is mentioned in Acts 16:1–9 and in 20:4, but in the third person. Neither Silas nor Titus are mentioned as accompanying Paul to Rome, nor are they referred to in his epistles written from prison. This would appear to leave only Luke as a possible writer of the we-sections. Quite appropriately, he does not refer to himself by name.

5. When we put these data together it emerges that

      a) The we-sections are an essential part of the history recorded in Acts.

      b) The writer of the we-sections is therefore the probable author of Acts.

      c) The we-sections bring Paul to the point of his Roman imprisonment.

      d) In three letters it is recorded that Luke was with Paul. In two of these letters the reference to Luke would appear to qualify him as the writer of the we-sections, there being no others who could qualify for that authorship.

This is the extent of the specifically New Testament evidence for the Lukan authorship of Acts. If Luke is the author of the we-sections and therefore of Acts as a whole, the same evidence would—in view of Acts 1:1 and Luke 1:1–4—apply to the authorship of the

gospel. No evidence has been presented that makes it possible se-
riously to question the correctness of the argument traced above or
of the tradition in the early church that Luke is the author of both
the third gospel and Acts.

On the more personal side, we know that Luke was a Gentile
and a physician (Col. 4:10–14). It is clear that Paul held him in the
highest esteem. Where he was born we do not know. His two books
reveal a man of high intelligence and cultural attainment, a man who
is devout, sympathetic to the poor and other unfortunates, and wholly
committed to the service of the gospel.

DATE AND PLACE OF WRITING

Neither Luke nor Acts contains information that makes it possible
to date their writing. If we make two assumptions, however, a reasonable effort can be made in the direction of dating Luke. The first
assumption is that the author used Mark as one of his major sources
of information. The second is that Luke, the companion of Paul, is
the author. The first is more than an assumption; it is accepted by
most New Testament scholars as an established fact. The second
assumption is as widely held as the first but not with the same
amount of evidence.

Mark, as we saw, probably wrote between A.D. 65 and 70. As
a close associate of Paul, Luke was undoubtedly well acquainted
with Mark who is mentioned by name in all three of Paul's references
to Luke. Although Mark, on our reckoning, wrote after the deaths
of Peter and Paul, it is reasonable to suppose that Luke remained
in touch with him. He may therefore have had access to Mark's
gospel soon after it was written. We do not know when Luke obtained his other sources, but in view of these suppositions and circumstances, a date between 70 and 75 for the writing of the gospel
is reasonable.

Nothing is known with even a small degree of certainty about
the place where Luke was written. Eusebius the historian and Jerome the Bible translator, whose lives spanned the larger part of the
fourth century, speak of the Antiochian origins of the gospel. Rome
and Alexandria have also been mentioned as possible centers where
Luke was written. It is wisest to hold no firm theory about the
question.

READERS

Luke was written for the information of "the most excellent Theophilus." Today we would say that Luke dedicated his book to him.

Many authors of antiquity dedicated their books to some eminent patron, and did so for various reasons. The dedication could be an expression of personal esteem and friendship. It could be motivated by the hope of receiving a reward for the honor that the dedication expressed. A third reason could be the desire to express gratitude for help of one kind or another that the patron had given to the author. However, we have no information leading us to believe that any of these reasons compelled our author to undertake so large a work as Luke-Acts represents.

A fourth reason is more probably the true one. The German New Testament scholar Theodore Zahn gave the following as a frequent reason for the dedication of books in the ancient world: ". . . from his patron's interest in the subject of the work or in the person of the author, the latter hoped to secure a wider circulation of his work; or because such a person seemed to him appropriately to represent the class of readers whom he desired to reach." In short, in dedicating his book to Theophilus, Luke may well have been motivated by a double reason. He may have hoped in this way to secure a wider interest in his book, and in the second place that it would receive the particular attention of a certain class of people in the empire.

There is a quite remarkable example of such a dedication on record in Jewish history. The Jewish historian Josephus dedicated his short work *Against Apion* in this way: ". . . but let this and the foregoing book be dedicated to thee, Epaphroditus, who art so great a lover of the truth and, by thy means, to those that have in like manner been desirous to be acquainted with the affairs of our nation." It is certainly reasonable to believe that Luke had a wider circle of readers in mind than one man and possibly some members of his family and a few friends. He therefore addressed it to some eminent or at all events highly respected person with an "interest in the subject of the work." He then hoped that this would introduce the book to "the class of readers" that a man like Theophilus seemed "appropriately to represent."

What kind of readers would this class of people consist of? If we know what kind of a man Theophilus was we shall have at least a general idea of the kind of people whom Luke tried to influence. Luke's purpose was "to write an orderly account for you, most excellent Theophilus, that you may know the truth concerning the things of which you have been informed" (1:3, 4). Two things stand out here: the address to Theophilus as "most excellent," and some indication of his relationship to Christianity. The Greek word *kra-*

tiste, translated "most excellent" is used by Luke on three other occasions, all in Acts (23:26; 24:3; 26:25). In each case it is applied in an official situation to a person in high office in the Roman government: twice to the governor, Felix, and once to his successor, Festus. It would seem, therefore, that the Theophilus of Luke 1:3 and Acts 1:1 had a very high social status so that he was properly addressed as *kratiste*. From this it may be concluded that he belonged to the Roman aristocracy, that he was a man of some influence, and that possibly he occupied a high office in the Roman government.

With respect to Christian commitment, Theophilus appears to have been what we would call today an inquirer. He had been "informed" of the truth of the gospel (1:4). That he had permitted himself to become informed is significant, for it indicates interest on his part. Luke seems to have entertained some doubt, however, about the accuracy of the information that he had received. He therefore wrote the gospel account in order that Theophilus may "know the truth" about what he had heard. The fact that Luke felt free to dedicate both of his books to Theophilus indicates that he had come to entertain a very definite interest in Christianity. At the same time, there is no suggestion that he had been instructed by the church, much less that he had received baptism. Finally, no conclusion can be drawn from the fact that his name was Theophilus, which means "friend of God." It was at the time a common name among both Jews and Gentiles.

There were many people like Theophilus in the Roman empire. They were weary of the coldness and formalism of state religion. They were too educated and cultured to accept the superstitions of traditional paganism. They were also too dissatisfied with the purely intellectual teachings of philosophy to accept them as the answer to their religious needs. Judaism was known in the ancient world and many respected it. But Gentiles were generally unwilling to surrender their Greek or Roman heritage to become Jews. Such feelings led many to be open to the Christian religion. In addressing Theophilus, Luke therefore addressed, as it were, this very large religiously hungry class of men and women in the empire.

In seeking to meet the needs of the Theophilus type of inquirer, however, Luke did not forget the needs either of Jews or of those who were already Christians. His undoubted knowledge of the Septuagint not only gave him a rich background in the Old Testament but, according to scholars, also gave a Semitic touch even to the style of his Greek writing. Christians needed to be better informed

about the life and work of Christ. The writing of Luke was occasioned by the needs of evangelism, but in meeting these he met no
less a deep need in the Christian community.

PURPOSE

We have already had occasion to note the evangelistic purpose of
the writing of Luke. We saw that it focused particularly on the
educated element in the Roman empire. This purpose we must now
consider in somewhat greater depth.

The empire was a most remarkable association of states, tribes,
cities, regions, and peoples ruled by its central government in Rome.
It stretched from England across Europe, North Africa, and the
Middle East to the Euphrates River in Mesopotamia. Doubtless Luke
had in mind the great society that peopled the empire when he wrote
his gospel. That he was well acquainted with it is shown by the
detailed list of nations in Acts 2. In Acts 1:8 he shows his sense of
evangelistic responsibility for it. It is therefore not surprising that
he should be concerned about the relationship between the church
and the empire.

When Luke wrote the gospel a very tragic period had begun in
the relations between Palestine and the empire. The Jews had re-
volted against Roman rule. They had been fearfully put down by
the Roman armies and Jerusalem "the beloved city" had been largely
destroyed. Luke appears to have been afraid that the Romans would
carry over their hostility to the church. While he does not openly
speak about it, his gospel gives evidence again and again of efforts
on his part to disarm any suspicion that Rome might have with
respect to the church or her faith.

Forty or so years earlier Jesus had been accused of being a
political trouble maker, and it was under Roman authority that he
had been crucified. In the early sixties Christians had been persecuted in Rome under Nero. Peter and Paul had been executed there.
With this in mind, and writing for a readership that is influential in
the empire, Luke wishes to relieve Roman fears of the Christian
religion. He seeks to do so by centering attention on Jesus, describing his peaceful intent, his purely religious and charitable motives,
and, not least of all, his innocence with respect to political agitation.
He was accused before Pilate of "perverting the nation and forbid-
ding us to give tribute to Caesar saying that he himself is Christ a
king" (23:2), but the Roman governor finds him innocent three times
(23:4, 13–16, 22). Under the pressure of Jewish leaders and people

he finally agrees to the crucifixion, for "their voices prevailed." In it all, however, the Roman government stands forth more as a protector of Jesus and as a tool of the Jews than as being guilty of injustice.

Further, Jesus' birth takes place in the reign of the greatest of the Romans, Caesar Augustus, and is related to his decree. When Jesus began his ministry Tiberius was Caesar and Pontius Pilate was governor of Judaea (3:1). The destruction of Jerusalem, which had probably taken place when Luke wrote, is not alluded to either in the gospel or in Acts. The lack of Roman interest in Christianity as a politically dangerous movement was later set forth dramatically in Acts 18:12-17.

It should further be noted how Luke presented Christ to such a varied society as was the Roman empire. He introduced him as the universal man. While Matthew traces Jesus' ancestry back to David and Abraham (1:1-6), and sees him as the fulfillment of Jewish hopes, Luke traces Jesus' ancestry back to Adam, the father of the human race. He was therefore to be the fulfillment of the hopes of humankind.

Luke's purpose, therefore, was to give a proper account, but with an evangelistic aim and intent, of the life and work of Jesus Christ. He wrote for a class of men such as that represented by Theophilus. He sought to remove Roman fears about the political character of the new religion. He emphasized the universality of the gospel. Meanwhile, the book is so written that it is of no small value for believers. That is, it is not simply a piece of missionary writing; rather, it is fully and truly a document of the church. From incarnation through a ministry of preaching, teaching, and healing, Luke leads his readers to the great climaxes of passion and resurrection, and closes with the Lord's command to preach the gospel to all nations, beginning with Jerusalem.

CHARACTERISTICS

Like Matthew and Mark, Luke has certain distinctive features that should be noted. We mention the following:

1. *BIRTH NARRATIVE*
While Matthew associates deep tragedy with Jesus' birth, Luke's account is joyful and elevating to the highest degree. Holy angels appear to simple shepherds and announce in song the birth of the Savior, which leads to reverent adoration in the stable. Mary is much

more prominent in Luke than in Matthew. The birth account in Luke is also set in the larger context of angelic announcements including that of the birth of John the Baptist, and there are psalm-like responses by Mary and Zacharias. In Luke the message of the incarnation is presented in incomparably beautiful and religiously moving description.

2. FOR ALL MEN

The universalism noted earlier is reenforced in various ways. In the angels' announcement the birth of Jesus has significance for all men (2:10–14). Jesus will be a light for revelation to the Gentiles (2:32). In various places (3:4–6; 14:23; 17:15–19; 24:47), Luke's vision of redemption extends far beyond Israel.

3. HUMAN CONCERN

In Luke, Jesus stands out as an intensely social being. Thirteen women not mentioned in other gospels are introduced by Luke. He has an eye for the sadness of life that can be felt but not expressed. For example, he tells us that the young man raised from the dead at Nain was "the only son of his mother, and she was a widow" (7:12). Jairus had "an only daughter, about twelve years of age, and she was dying" (8:42). Such passages show a deep understanding of tragedy. Furthermore, Jesus' discussion with Cleopas and his companion on the day of resurrection is unforgettable (24:13–35). Jesus' openness to Zacchaeus, his association with the poor and the outcast, his sympathy with poverty, and his criticism of the rich all stand out markedly in Luke.

4. JESUS AT PRAYER

Jesus appears as a man of prayer more in Luke than in Matthew and Mark. Nine times and under varying circumstances, from the time of his baptism to his death on the cross, Jesus is reported as praying or has having prayed (3:21; 5:16; 6:12; 9:18; 9:28; 11:1; 22:32; 22:41; 23:34). Luke has three parables on prayer that are not found in Matthew or Mark: the friend coming at midnight (11:5–8); the unjust judge (18:1–8); and the pharisee and the publican (18:9–14).

5. THE SERMON ON THE PLAIN

Jesus' Sermon on the Mount, so extensively reported in Matthew, also appears in Luke but in greatly altered form. Matthew's Sermon, including two introductory and two concluding verses, consists of 111 verses of unbroken teaching in chapters 5, 6, and 7. Luke has only 54 verses parallel to Matthew's material. Of these, 24 are found in Luke 6:20–49. At the time he spoke these words, Jesus was standing "on a level place" (6:17), and the passage is therefore known as the "Sermon on the Plain." The remaining 30 verses are spread over chapters 11, 12, 13, 14, and 16 in ten single or small groups of verses. The longest continuous passage running parallel with Matthew is 12:22–32 (cf. Matt. 6:25–34).

6. TWO LITERARY PECULIARITIES

One of the most outstanding features of Luke on the literary side is Jesus' long return journey from Galilee to Jerusalem, which extends from 9:51 to 19:27. This long interlude of some ten chapters has no chronological order. In 9:51 Jesus and his disciples depart from Galilee to go to Jerusalem. In 10:38 they reach the home of Mary and Martha, close to Jerusalem. In 17:11 they are passing along between Samaria and Galilee, which is near to where they began their journey. Because Luke's account departs altogether from the Markan order from 9:51 to 18:14, the material lying in between has been called the Great Insertion.

The return journey is no less remarkable for its content than for its unusual length. It has a great deal of material found neither in Matthew nor in Mark, such as the parables of the Good Samaritan, the Rich Fool, the Lost Sheep, the Lost Coin, the Prodigal Son, the Unjust Steward, and the Rich Man and Lazarus. For this as well as for other aspects it is a very rich part of the gospel as a whole.

A second peculiarity is noticeable only to the student of the Synoptic Problem (cf. Chapter VII). Luke draws freely on Mark, using about fifty percent of it. This fifty percent is drawn from the book as a whole, however, and not from any one section of it. It is therefore strange that Luke uses no material at all from Mark 6:45 to 8:10. This absence in Luke has been called the Great Omission.

7. THE BIRTH ACCOUNT

Like Matthew and unlike Mark and John, Luke has a birth account of Jesus. In common with Matthew, it has the central feature of the Virgin Birth in Bethlehem. In almost all other respects the birth stands in a wholly different context of events. This suggests that Matthew and Luke obtained their respective data from different sources.

STRUCTURE

As in Mark, the material presented by Luke does not permit any logical structuring. Indeed, the Great Insertion makes it even more difficult to organize Luke's material than Mark's. Geographical division is the only suitable way of outlining the book. We have noted before that the similarity between the three gospels is most strongly expressed geographically. The structural unity that characterizes all three is Jesus' baptism and temptation in Judea, his ministry in Galilee, his return journey to Judea, and finally his passion, death, and resurrection in Jerusalem. To this basic pattern Luke has added an extensive birth account, substantial details of the return journey to Jerusalem (considerable material that is found in neither Matthew nor Mark), and the very significant prologue.

The resultant structural outline of Luke is then as follows:

I. The Prologue (1:1–4)
II. The Birth of Jesus (1:15–2:52)
III. Introduction by John the Baptist, Baptism, Genealogy, Temptation (3:1–4:13)
IV. Ministry in Galilee (4:14–9:50)
V. Return to Jerusalem (9:51–19:27)
VI. Ministry in Jerusalem (19:28–21:38)
VII. Last Supper, Passion, Resurrection (22:1–24:53)

CHAPTER VI

HIGHER CRITICISM

In the study of Matthew, Mark, and Luke we noted the characteristic feature of similarities and differences between them. How this unusual feature of similarities/differences came into being (i.e., the Synoptic Problem) has been the focus of a very special study by New Testament scholars.

Before studying this problem, however, it is most desirable to have at least an elementary understanding of the method that Bible scholars employ in analyzing scriptural data. Known as higher criticism, this method is used not only in the study of the Synoptics, but also in the study of all other books of the Bible. Higher criticism has a companion discipline known as lower criticism. Together these two disciplines are known as biblical criticism.

There is a great deal of misunderstanding about designating the study of the Bible as "criticism." Is it not irreverent to criticize the Bible? And why is one kind of criticism called "higher," while another "lower"? Let us therefore first try to understand what is meant by "criticism," and then what is meant by "lower" and "higher" criticism.

In everyday English, "criticism" usually has a negative, unfavorable significance. We do not enjoy being "criticized." The word "criticism" also has, however, another and very important meaning. The English word is derived from the Greek word *krinein*, which, in addition to a negative meaning, has a positive meaning, namely, "to choose," "to prefer," "to estimate," "to evaluate," or "to make a judgment upon a matter." A *krites* in ancient Greece was a discerner, a judge, an arbiter. Specifically in Athens, the center of Greek culture, he was a judge of poetic contests. Today we speak of literary critics, music critics, and art critics. In all such criticism the basic movement is positive and appreciative rather than negative and condemnatory. In short, criticism of this kind seeks to evaluate a matter as to its character, be it a novel, a piece of music, or a work of art.

It is precisely in this way that the discipline of biblical criticism studies the books of the Bible. Lower criticism seeks to determine the exact words or text in which the books of the Bible were written. It tries to ascertain as nearly as possible the very words that the writer used in the original manuscript. For this reason lower criticism is usually called textual criticism. It analyzes and compares, especially in the area of New Testament research, the many ancient handwritten copies of New Testament books that have been discovered over the centuries. The original writings, now lost, are called autographa, that is, books written by the author's own hand. The most illustrious example of the fruit of such criticism is the vast improvement in accuracy of modern versions of the Bible such as the Revised Standard Version or the New English Bible as compared with the King James Version. The RSV and NEB are based on manuscripts some of which were copied as early as the fourth century, while the KJV was based on manuscripts that were copied in the tenth and twelfth centuries. As a result of its help in modern translations, one seldom hears any unfavorable judgments about lower or textual criticism.

Higher criticism is probably called "higher" because it works with the basic or "lower" text that is determined by textual criticism. It seeks to understand the books of the Bible individually and in relation to each other, in the light of historical, cultural, religious, political, and other contexts within which they were written. For this reason higher criticism has various distinct though closely related branches of study. These are:

1. SOURCE CRITICISM

This kind of higher criticism seeks to ascertain and evaluate the sources that the author of a given book used in writing it. As an example of the reasonableness of such criticism we may cite Luke 1:1–3. There the writer speaks of the things that "were delivered to us by those who from the beginning were eyewitnesses and ministers of the word." These led him, "having followed all things closely for some time past, to write an orderly account of them." In our study of the Synoptic gospels it will become clear that the gospel of Mark was one of these sources and that in Matthew and in Luke there are clear pointings to at least three other sources.

2. HISTORICAL CRITICISM

This branch of higher criticism is concerned with studying the historical aspects of a given book. It tries to see these aspects in relation to each other within the book, to other books in the Bible by the same author, to books by other writers, and to the secular history of the time. Archaeology plays an important role here. Through the investigation of ancient ruins, the study of artifacts found in them, and of inscriptions of various kinds, much knowledge has come to light that greatly helps us to understand the situation in which the authors of the Bible wrote.

3. *LITERARY CRITICISM*

This aspect of higher criticism has been and probably will remain the most important of all. It investigates questions that have to do with a given book as a piece of writing. Who is its author? To whom or for whom did he write? Did the book have a single or a multiple authorship? If the latter, who was the editor or editors who brought together the final version we now have? When was the book written? What are its characteristic features? What are its contents and how are they structured? What is its relationship to other books in the canon?

It is unavoidable that literary, source, and historical criticism should interact with each other even though each will retain its own character. Higher criticism is of one piece, its various branches are branches of one tree.

The most recent arrivals on the higher critical scene are form criticism and redaction criticism. Of these the former is the more significant. Because of its contemporary significance, and especially its bearing on the Synoptic Problem, we shall devote a more extended discussion to this branch of higher criticism.

4. *FORM CRITICISM*

The chapter on the Synoptic Problem will show that a) Mark was the first of the Synoptics to be written, b) both Matthew and Luke used Mark as a major source, c) an additional unidentified source known as Q was used by Matthew and Luke, d) Matthew drew on an unidentified source known as M for material found neither in Mark nor in Luke, and finally e) Luke drew on an unidentified source known as L for material found neither in Mark nor in Matthew. What form criticism tries to do is to penetrate behind Mark and Q and M and L to discover the nature of these sources and how they came into being.

It would seem that what we have here is a case of source criticism. Why then is it called form criticism? We have noticed in the reading of the gospels that the same parables, sayings, teachings, miracles, and narratives about Jesus may appear in sequences or contexts that often differ in the three gospels. The time, the place, the relation to what precedes or follows, and the participants or people addressed may vary, with respect to the same data, from gospel to gospel. This circumstance has led the form critics to the theory that much or all of the data found in the Synoptics circulated orally in the circles of Jesus' followers before any of the gospels were written. That is, it circulated in the Christian community in the *form* of short sayings, teachings, narratives, parables, and accounts of miracles. The church community, so the form critics continue, refined and gave more definite *form* to these accounts. It did this particularly in view of the needs and problems that it faced, notably in preaching, teaching, church discipline, relations to the local and Roman authorities, worship, marriage and divorce, church administration, defense of the gospel, and similar matters.

Especially in societies in which the ability to read is not widespread, tradition is transmitted and given body in definite oral or verbal *forms*. It was in this manner, the form critics say, that the tradition about Jesus was remembered in the early church. As the apostles who knew Jesus most intimately aged and died, the oral tradition was committed to writing and at last found permanent and recognized expression in the gospels. One of the earliest aspects to find a common account in the church was the passion narrative with the sequence of last supper, betrayal, arrest, trial, crucifixion, death, burial, and resurrection of Jesus.

Form criticism therefore seeks to determine a) the earliest forms, that is, the verbal or oral forms, in which the gospel circulated in the church, and b) the contexts in which these forms were meaningful in the life, witness, and service of the church. Different scholars give different names to the several forms in which the gospel is thought to have circulated. Perhaps the clearest list is given by the British form critic Vincent Taylor. His major classifications are: a) Pronouncement Stories, b) Sayings, c) Parables, d) Miracle Narratives, and e) Narrative material about Jesus not covered in the material a–d. We shall characterize these briefly.

a) Pronouncement Stories

In these accounts the emphasis lies on the word "pronouncement." It is a saying of Jesus that the church remembered and placed in the context of a situation in which he is presented as having delivered it. A good example is Mark 12:13–17. The story part exists in order to provide an occasion or framework to the pronouncement part, which is, "Render to Caesar the things that are Caesar's and to God the things that are God's." Other instances are Luke 9:57–62; Matt. 19:13–15; Mark 2:15–17; 2:23–28; 3:31–35; 6:1–4. In all of these the description of the situation is said to be subordinate to Jesus' short but significant pronouncement.

b) Sayings

There are many other pronouncements or sayings of Jesus that do not have a situation account associated with them. These are for purposes of distinction called Sayings. There is a great amount of this material in the Synoptics. Many are short statements of only one or two lines. Others may form a substantial paragraph. The Sermon on the Mount (Matt. 5–7) consists of this kind of sayings. More often, however, the sayings have not been gathered into the form of one long discourse as in the Sermon on the Mount. The material called Sayings of Jesus may be classified as follows with accompanying examples:

i.   *Wisdom Sayings*: Matt. 5:4–12; Luke 6:31; 9:40
ii. *Legal Sayings and Church Rules*: Matt. 5:34–37; 12:11, 12; 18:15–17; 18:18
iii. *Prophetic and Apocalyptic Sayings*: Matt. 11:20–24; 23:37–39; Luke 11:49–50; Mark 13:1–37
iv. *Sayings About Himself*: Matt. 11:4–6; 12:40; 18:20; Mark 8:38; Luke 12:49–51; 17:25

c) Parables, which are readily recognizable

d) Accounts of Miracles

Usually there are three elements in a miracle account:

i.   the situation in which the miracle is performed
ii. a description of the miraculous act
iii. the consequences of the miracle

The typical miracle story is well illustrated in the double miracle account in Mark 5:21–43.

e) Narrative Material About Jesus

This material represents accounts about Jesus himself that circulated in the early church emphasizing Jesus' character and deeds. In due course these were included in the written gospels.

The way in which form critics *classify* the data found in the Synoptics as listed above varies from one author to another. Nevertheless, there is an overall fairly general agreement about classification of data. In contrast, there are great differences in the manner in which form critics *interpret* the data that they classify. In this

respect there is no general area of agreement at all. It is necessary
to realize this if the deeper significance of form criticism is to be
understood. The earliest form critics, Bultmann and Dibelius, both
German scholars, had a very low opinion of the gospels with respect
to their historical value. In their view little is known of the actual
Jesus who walked among men in Judea and Galilee nearly two thousand years ago. What we have in the gospels, they say, are accounts
of sayings and deeds that are *attributed* to Jesus, but that have relatively little basis in what he actually said and did. As the church
and the Christian community found themselves confronted by many
problems and new situations they somehow fashioned parables, laws,
sayings, teachings, and accounts of miracles to meet these situations
and problems, and attributed them to Jesus. Questions about the
sabbath, marriage and divorce, taxation, baptism, worship, the giving of alms, discipline, and relations of the Church to Pharisees,
Saducees, and the Roman government were all dealt with by means
of accounts of deeds and teachings that were ascribed to Jesus but
were in fact the product of the Christian community. It is not denied
that Jesus lived and taught and did great works, but how much of
this history is actually represented by the accounts in the gospels
is quite another matter. This view was adopted by many later form
critics who again differ much among themselves. What one may
consider to be a true saying or deed of Jesus another will attribute
to the Christian community. Still other form critics accept the classification of data, but see the data as based on actual words and
deeds of Jesus. A summary is therefore in order about the weak-
nesses and strengths of form criticism.

Weaknesses of Form Criticism

i. The earliest form critics have been sharply criticized by more
recent New Testament scholars for attributing many or most of the
deeds and words of Jesus to the devout imagination of the church.
That the words and deeds of Jesus himself should be soon forgotten
and that the church thereupon should create sayings attributed to
him, and fashion stories about him, does not seem to be warranted
by the facts. When the gospels began to be written many who had
known Jesus in the flesh were still alive. Why should they not remember the living context in which Jesus spoke and acted? Why
should the church remember only some outstanding sayings of Jesus?

ii. Books are not written by communities but by individual
people. These individual people are members of the community and
absorb what they hear in the community. But in the process of

absorbing what they hear they also sort out, sift, compare, and test in order to obtain the facts about a matter. It is most unlikely that in the short space of four or five decades the church should have forgotten or become indifferent to the facts of Jesus' person and ministry, and in their place brought into being a full-fledged complex of stories, miracles, sayings, and parables that it attributed to him, but that formed no part of his actual words and deeds.

In the gospels and Acts the apostolate of twelve men plays a very great role. They had been with Jesus throughout his ministry, they had seen and heard all that he did and said, and they had themselves been instructed by him. What they wrote or what some of their assistants wrote was a deposit of remembered acts and words of Jesus and of circumstances and situations in which he had been involved.

iii. The attempt to classify all the data in the Synoptics that bear on Jesus, especially his sayings and teachings, often leads to arbitrariness and artificiality. Jesus' teachings, miracles, wisdom, sayings, parables, and not least all that he says about himself are so intertwined and interrelated that separating and isolating their individual parts is a dissection that tends to take the life out of the whole.

iv. Form criticism is concerned with discovering the original verbal *forms* of narratives, parables, miracle stories, and so forth. But when the form critic begins to judge what Jesus said and did, and what Jesus did not say and do, then he is not really a *form* critic anymore, but has become a *historical* critic. It was pointed out earlier that the various critical disciplines are interrelated, that they need and use each other. But there are limits to this interplay, and the following point indicates how far form criticism has gone beyond its own proper area.

v. The most serious judgment that must be made on the early and, to an extent, continuing form criticism relates to the distinction that it makes between the "earthly Jesus" and the "Christ of faith." Form criticism professes to know very little about Jesus' earthly life. What we read about Jesus in the gospels may not at all, in its view, represent actual history and actual teaching. But it does not regard this as important. What *is* important in form critical theory is the product of the church's reflection and devout imagination about Jesus. This product deals not with the historical Jesus but with the "Christ of faith." It is he, not the "Jesus of history," who is the object of the church's belief and hope.

This decided distinction between Jesus as a human being and

Christ as a religious idea is not warranted by New Testament teaching. In it, the names Jesus and Christ refer to one and the same
person. "And Jesus asked his disciples . . . 'Who do men say that
I am?' . . . Peter answered him, 'You are the Christ' " (Mark
8:27–29); and so throughout the New Testament. True, the name
"Christ," representing Jesus' messianic office and frequently referring to his preincarnate state, vastly enriches Jesus' person. But the
two are never separated. In form criticism the rootage of the "Christ
of faith" is not the person of Jesus, the incarnate Son of God who
lived, taught, suffered, died and rose again from the dead. Rather,
the "Christ of faith" is an idea or ideal that exists only in the mind
of the church. It is true that in form critical teaching the "Jesus of
history" inspired the idea of the "Christ of faith," but in actual fact
the "Christ of faith" never had historical existence.

It is considerations such as these that have brought form criticism into ill repute in many sections of the church. Many feel like
Mary at the tomb of Jesus, "They have taken away my Lord and I
do not know where they have laid him." This may not, however,
deter us from appreciating and using those substantial elements in
form criticism that are helpful in achieving a better understanding
of how the gospels came into being. The theological disciplines of
doctrine and exegesis can be used in a negative as well as in a
positive way. This does not, however, lead us to abandon the use of
doctrine and exegesis in the pursuit of theology. So it is with form
criticism and with all other aspects of higher criticism.

The Value of Form Criticism

Like higher criticism in general, form criticism helps us to
understand the thoroughly human way in which God was pleased
to give us the gospels. When one chapter in a book consists entirely
of parables, another of miracles, and still others exclusively of teachings, it is clear that a grouping of materials has taken place which
in all probability was not so experienced in Jesus' day-to-day ministry. Similarly, when one writer describes a given event in one way
and another writer places the same event in a quite different context
of time and place, and even in wording alters the meaning of the
first account, it is clear that each had a different structuring of the
event in mind than the other. And again, it is entirely reasonable to
suppose that the writers of the gospels focused the teachings and
deeds of Jesus upon the needs and problems that the Church faced
at the time they wrote.

Form criticism, insofar as it has remained true to its character as dealing with *forms* of teachings and narratives, has rendered a genuine service in showing *how* the good new of salvation, as given to and remembered by the church, received the literary structures that now lie before us in the gospels.

5. *REDACTION CRITICISM*

Form criticism leads to redaction criticism. Of this type of biblical criticism we must take brief note. A redactor is an editor. The word "editor" is mainly used in two senses today. When associated with a newspaper or magazine, an editor is a person who comments on the news and affairs of the day. When he is associated with a publishing house an editor prepares acceptable manuscripts for publication. It is editing or redaction in this latter sense that best points the way to an understanding of what is meant by redaction in biblical criticism.

The men who wrote the Synoptic gospels were proper writers or authors. It is clear, however, as we shall see more fully in the next chapter, that in their writing they used various sources. Both Mark and Q served Matthew and Luke as sources, and the sources M and L served Matthew and Luke separately. What source or sources Mark used we do not know, but it can hardly be doubted that he too had access to needed information.

The work of selecting materials from available sources and integrating those materials into the structure of a book may properly be called editing or redacting. The study of the way in which the synoptists performed this editorial work in the writing of their individual gospels is called redaction criticism. In the study of the Synoptics the service rendered by redaction criticism is of particular value because of the varied use that the writers make of the same data.

CHAPTER VII

THE SYNOPTIC PROBLEM

The separate studies of Matthew, Mark, and Luke bring us now to consider them in their relationship to each other. Having read the three gospels, we should be impressed with the remarkable similarities that exist between them. At the same time, we have noticed the extensive differences that are no less apparent. Sometimes these differences appear within the very similarities, as when the same event or teaching is described in different words or from differing points of view. For example, both Matthew and Luke have much teaching material spoken by Jesus. But in Matthew this material is carefully structured, while in Luke there is no discernible organization of it. Mark, on the other hand, is predominantly a narrative of events, even though it has a substantial amount of teaching material. Nevertheless, whether one reads one gospel or the other, he definitely feels that the subject matter, the moods and responses it creates in the reader, the various people and experiences that are met in the reading, and above all the central figure of Jesus, are of one piece. There is good reason for calling each of these gospels The Gospel.

It is this combination of circumstances that has given to these three gospels a common name by which they are known in the area of New Testament scholarship: "the Synoptics." This name is derived from the Greek word *sunoptikos*, which means "common view" or "viewed together." The many questions that this "viewing together" raises are collectively known as "the Synoptic Problem," the foremost problem in New Testament study. In this chapter we shall consider the main outlines of this problem.

THE PROBLEM OUTLINED

The resemblances and the differences that we meet in the Synoptics are by no means all of one kind. There are various types of similarities and various types of differences. We shall note these separately and then illustrate them by means of parallel quotations from the gospels.

1. *KINDS OF SIMILARITIES*

a) Passages common to all three gospels

We have noted again and again that ninety percent of the material that is found in Mark is also found, in one way or another, in Matthew; and similarly that fifty percent of Mark is found in Luke. Specifically, there are no less than ninety-three passages of common material, although of varying length, that are found in all three of the gospels.

b) Passages common to two gospels

Matthew and Mark have twelve passages in common that are not found in Luke. There are only four passages found in Mark and Luke that are not found in Matthew. Two of these involve the questionable part of Mark 16. There is also a remarkable correspondence between Matthew and Luke in which Mark plays no role. They have twenty-eight passages in common covering more than 200 verses in each book.

c) Numbers of common passages

If, therefore, we designate Matthew, Mark, and Luke by the letters A, B, and C respectively, we discover the following combinations of common material: ABC have ninety-three passages in common; AB twelve passages; AC twenty-eight passages, and BC four passages.

d) Similarities in wording

In many passages there is wording that is virtually identical with that of the corresponding passages in other books. Twenty, thirty, or more consecutive words may show little or no difference whether in the words themselves or in their order in the sentence.

e) Similarity in structure

All three gospels have a common basic structure, which is found most clearly in Mark. It consists of Jesus' preparation in Judea, his ministry in Galilee, his return to Judea, his ministry in Judea and Jerusalem, and finally his arrest, passion, death, and resurrection.

f) Priority of the Marcan order

The order in which the material is arranged in Matthew and Luke is in large measure determined by the order in Mark. (Cf. the list of passages at the end of this chapter that indicates the unbroken order in Mark.)

2. *KINDS OF DIFFERENCES*

a) In historical setting

The same matter may be found in a different context of time, occasion, and agents in one gospel than in another. A striking example of this is Matthew 20:20–28; Mark 10:35–45; Luke 22:24–27.

b) In literary structure and character of the contents

The literary structure of Matthew is quite different, as we have noted, from that of either Mark or Luke. Moreover, Mark differs from both Matthew and Luke in that he presents mainly narrative material. Luke differs from Matthew and Mark in the long travel account of Jesus' return from Galilee to Jerusalem, which extends from 9:51 to 18:14. Mark has no genealogy or birth account of Jesus. Matthew and Luke have both, but they are markedly dissimilar to each other.

c) In wording and historical detail

The same matter may in varying degrees be differently reported as to literary and historical presentation.

d) In meaning

The same matter may be reported with substantial difference in meaning by giving different functions to identical words. Note especially the parallel passages of the story of the rich young ruler below.

3. *EXAMPLES OF SIMILARITIES AND DIFFERENCES IN PARALLEL PASSAGES*

In the examples that follow it will be observed how complex and pervasive are the above-mentioned similarities and differences. This can be seen only, however, when the parallel passages are closely read, reread, and compared. An illustration is offered of such comparison under the first example. In all the passages significant differences are underlined.

a) Same occasion with differences in words and word order

Matt. 3:11	Mark 1:7, 8	Luke 3:16
I baptize you with water *for repentance*, but he who is coming after me is mightier than I, *whose sandals* I am not worthy *to carry*; he will baptize you with the Holy Spirit and *with fire*.	After me comes one who is mightier than I, the *thong* of whose sandals I am not worthy to *stoop down* and untie. I *have baptized* you with water; but he will baptize you with the Holy Spirit.	I baptize you with water; but he who is mightier than I *is coming*, the thong of whose sandals I am not worthy to untie; he will baptize you with the Holy Spirit and with fire.

Sample Analysis:

i. In Matthew and Luke, John's "I baptize you with water" appears first. In Mark, his "I have baptized you with water" appears at the end.

ii. Only Matthew has "for repentance."

iii. The grammar of the context in which "mightier than I" stands is different in each case.

iv. In Matthew, John is not worthy to *carry Jesus' sandals*. In Luke, he is not worthy to *untie the thong* of Jesus' sandals; in Mark, he is not worthy to *stoop down* and untie the thong of Jesus' sandals.

v. In Matthew and Luke, Jesus will baptize "with the Holy Spirit and with fire." In Mark "and with fire" is not given.

vi. In Matthew and Luke the baptism of John and the baptism of Jesus are separated by the sandals reference. In Mark they are joined.

In spite of all these rather striking differences the content and message of all three are the same, namely, the superiority of Jesus' baptism over that of John.

b) Difference in subject of action

Matthew 8:5–13	Luke 7:1–10
And as he entered Capernaum, *a centurion came forward to him*, beseeching him and saying,	After he had ended all his sayings in the hearing of the people, he entered Capernaum. Now a centurion had a slave who was dear to him, who was sick and at the point of death. When he heard of Jesus *he sent to him elders of the Jews*, asking him to come and heal his slave. And when they came to Jesus, they besought him earnestly, saying, He is worthy to have you do this for him, for he loves our nation, and he built us our synagogue. And Jesus went
Lord, my servant is lying paralyzed at home, in terrible distress.	
And he said to him, I will come and heal him. *But the centurion answered him*, Lord, I am not worthy to have you come under my roof . . .	with them. When he was not far from the house, *the centurion sent friends to him*, saying to him, Lord do not trouble yourself, for I am not worthy. . . .

c) Change of reference in one book; omission in two

Matt. 19:16, 17, 19, 20	Mark 10:17, 18, 20, 21	Luke 18:18–21
And, behold, one came up to him, saying	And as he was setting out on his journey, a man ran up and knelt before him, and asked him,	And a ruler asked him

Teacher, *what good deed must I do* to have eternal life? And he said to him, *Why do you ask me about what is good? One there is who is good.* If you would enter life, keep the commandments . . . The young man said to him, All these things have I observed; what do I still lack? Jesus said to him, If you would be perfect, go, sell what you possess and give to the poor . . .

Good teacher, what must I do to inherit eternal life? And Jesus said to him, *Why do you call me good? No one is good but God alone.* You know the commandments . . .

And he said to him, Teacher, all these have I observed from my youth. *And Jesus looking upon him loved him*, and said to him, You lack one thing; go, sell what you have, and give to the poor . . .

Good teacher, what shall I do to inherit eternal life? And Jesus said to him, *Why do you call me good? No one is good but God alone.* You know the commandments . . .

And he said, All these have I observed from my youth. And when Jesus heard it he said to him, One thing you still lack. Sell all that you have and distribute to the poor . . .

In these passages it is especially important to note the altogether different reference that Matthew gives to the adjective "good" in the first two uses than Mark and Luke do.

d) Changes in place and number

Matt. 20:29, 30
And *as they went out* of Jericho, a great crowd followed him. And, behold, *two blind men* sitting by the roadside, when they heard that Jesus was passing by, cried out . . .

Mark 10:46, 47
And they *came to Jericho;* and as *he was leaving Jericho* with his disciples and a great multitude, *Bartimaeus, a blind beggar, son of Timaeus*, was sitting by the roadside. And when he heard that it was Jesus of Nazareth, he began to cry out . . .

Luke 18:35–38
And *as he drew near to Jericho, a blind man* was sitting by the roadside begging; and hearing a multitude going by, he inquired what this meant. They told him Jesus of Nazareth is passing by. And he cried . . .

e) Addition of exceptive clause in one book

Matt. 19:9 (5:32)
But I say to you that everyone who divorces his wife, *except on the ground of unchastity*, makes her an adulteress; and whoever marries a divorced woman commits adultery (cf. also 5:32).

Mark 10:11, 12
And he said to them, whoever divorces his wife and marries another, commits adultery against her; and if she divorces her husband and marries another, she commits adultery.

Luke 16:18
Everyone who divorces his wife and marries another commits adultery, and he who marries a woman divorced from her husband commits adultery.

The above examples constitute only a few of the many to be found in the Synoptic gospels. Only the most striking differences have been noted. A careful reading will reveal a number of minor differences, especially in wording. It is hardly possible to notice these similarities and differences by casual reading. Careful cross-referencing in the same Bible or even in different Bibles lying open at the parallel passages helps, but is still difficult. The only effective way to read the parallel passages is to read them in a harmony of the gospels. For this, H. F. D. Sparks' *A Synopsis of the Gospels* (Part I, Second Edition, 1970) is highly recommended. (Sparks' edition has the further advantage of taking note of Johannine parallels.) Even this method, however, does not reveal the full scope of existing similarities and divergences. To see them in their fullest dimension it is necessary to consult a harmony (or synopsis) of the three gospels in Greek.

HISTORY OF THE SYNOPTIC PROBLEM

Obviously, these similarities and differences are not accidental, and lead the serious student to look for an explanation. The problem is by no means a modern discovery. About A.D. 170 Tatian, probably a Syrian Christian, composed a single version of the gospels (including John) called the *Diatessaron* (meaning "the Fourfold"). We do not know in which language it was originally written; ancient versions of it exist in Arabic, Armenian, and Latin. Its purpose was to blend all the gospels into one book. This Tatain did with considerable skill, weaving passages ranging from parts of a verse to whole paragraphs into one continuous account divided into fifty-five sections. In the process he eliminated approximately one fourth of the verses, nearly all of them from Matthew, Mark, and Luke. Below follows a sample passage about the death of John the Baptist, with text references in the margin:

And his disciples came and took his body, and buried it.	Mk. 6:29
And they came and told Jesus what had happened. And for	Mt. 14:12
this cause Herod said, I beheaded John: who is this of	Lk. 9:9
whom I hear these things? And he desired to see him. And	
Jesus, when he had heard, removed thence in a boat to a	Mt. 13:14[a]
waste place alone, to the other side of the	Jo. 6:1[b]
Sea of Galilee of Tiberius.	

In course of time the church abandoned the use of the *Diatessaron*, and the four gospels continued to stand in their own right.

But the idea that it had stood for, namely, that of one combined gospel, has never fully left the church. For most Christians the gosples are a blur of stories and teachings. Only a few of these, like the Sermon on the Mount and the accounts of Jesus' birth, stand identified in their minds with particular gospels. In the sixteenth century even as great a theologian as John Calvin wrote a commentary on Matthew, Mark, and Luke in which all similar passages were printed together. He interpreted them as a unit and paid little attention to the differences between them. This commentary has a long history of use in the church.

There has always been greater or less concern to understand the interrelationship between the first three gospels. John stands in a class by itself—for which there are indeed good reasons. St. Augustine regarded Matthew as the original of the first three gospels. Mark was considered to be a sort of digest of it, and Luke was regarded as a gospel that drew material from both Matthew and Mark. This was the general view until modern times.

In the eighteenth and nineteenth centuries new theories developed. The following four views came into being:

a) Some held that an original gospel had been written in Aramaic, the language of Palestine, and that Matthew, Mark, and Luke all used it as a source, each in his own way.

b) Another view held that the apostles wrote accounts of Jesus' words and deeds that were used in the mission to the Gentiles. Collections were made of these in the Greek language, and in due course they formed the basis for the writing of the present canonical gospels.

c) A number of scholars attached a great deal of importance to oral tradition. Many accounts of Jesus' life, they held, were handed down by word of mouth through the telling of stories, through instruction, and in preaching. Originally this was done in Aramaic, but as the gospel spread these accounts were rendered into Greek. The Greek version in due course became the basis for the writing of the gospels. This view is especially represented by B. F. Westcott, the British biblical scholar.

d) Out of these efforts to understand the interrelationships of the Synoptics developed important views about the sources of the Synoptics—views that form the basis of synoptic study to this day. They center around the character and function of the sources known as Mark, Q, M, and L. Together these provide a very reasonable explanation of the similarities and differences that constitute the Synoptic Problem. Briefly stated, the situation today is as follows:

All synoptic study has as its starting point the assumption that there is a fundamental literary relationship between the three gospels. One gospel has drawn from another. The question then arises: which gospel was prior to the other two, thereby becoming a source for the writing of the others? If other sources were also used, how shall these sources be identified or described? The attention that has been given to these questions has produced several broad areas of agreement:

a) The basic gospel of the three is Mark. He wrote before Matthew and Luke did, and both drew extensively from him. There are definite reasons for believing in this priority of Mark, and we shall note them below. At this point we merely describe the present state of the question. Its cornerstone is that of Marcan priority.

b) There is much material that Matthew and Luke have in common that is not found in Mark. It constitutes some 230 verses in Matthew and somewhat over 200 in Luke, and consists almost entirely of discourse material. In view of the remarkable similarity between these large segments in Matthew and in Luke, they are regarded as having a common source also. A German scholar gave the name Q to this assumed source, Q being the first letter in the German word *Quelle*, a word which means "source." The use of the letter Q (like the use of x and y in algebra) implies that the source is not known. Unlike Mark, it does not have concrete literary existence. Moreover, there is no direct evidence that such a source, whether oral or written, ever existed. Q is a source that is assumed to have existed on the ground of striking similarities in Matthew and Luke while, at the same time, this material is absent in Mark. It is further assumed that both Matthew and Luke had access to this source and used it, together with Mark's gospel, to write their own distinctive gospels.

c) We note, in the third place, material that is not common at all but is found only in Matthew or only in Luke. Outstanding in this material are the differing stories about the birth of Jesus, considerable discourse material in Matthew, a substantial part of Luke's travel account (9:51–18:14), and several events in their respective passion and resurrection narratives, notably Luke 24. A number of sayings in Matthew are regarded as coming from an unknown "sayings" source that has been named M. Most of the special material in Luke has been designated as deriving from a source called L. The places given to M and L in the theory of sources are the least certain of the four sources considered.

In broad lines, this is the way in which the distinctive similarities and differences characterizing the Synoptics are accounted for.

OBSERVATIONS ON SOURCES AND ON THE PRIORITY OF MARK

1. *OBSERVATION ON SOURCES*

It must be clearly understood by the beginning student that the letters M and L do *not* refer to the gospels of Matthew and Luke. They refer to *sources* that may have been used in the writing of Matthew and Luke. The M source supplied much of the material in Matthew that is found neither in Mark nor in Luke. The L source supplied much of the material in Luke that is found neither in Mark nor in Matthew. As in the case of Q, there is no evidence that these sources actually existed. The absence of evidence for the existence of sources does not mean, however, that they did not exist, or are purely imaginary things in the minds of biblical scholars. The nature of the Synoptics makes the use of sources in their composition a wholly reasonable likelihood. If Matthew and Mark found so much common narrative material in Mark, why should they not derive common discourse material from another source? And why should they not draw their distinctive Matthean and Lukan material from still other sources?

Certainty about sources will never be attained until they are found, and that, at this late date, is extremely unlikely. At the same time, the solution set forth here for the Synoptic Problem is not universally shared. Especially in the Roman Catholic tradition there is a strong line of scholarly support for the priority of Matthew. This has bearing on the authorship of sources, but it does not alter the likelihood of sources as such. Any doubt that is held about them must always keep in mind Luke's own words, "Inasmuch as many have undertaken to compile a narrative of the things which have been accomplished among us, just as they were delivered to us by those who from the beginning were eyewitnesses and ministers of the word, it seemed good to me also, having followed all things closely, to write an orderly account . . ." (1:1–3).

2. *OBSERVATION ON THE PRIORITY OF MARK*

We have observed several times that all three gospels have the same basic structure regarding the stages of Jesus' ministry. We also saw that this comes to clearest expression in Mark. A similar and even more striking situation obtains with respect to the order of separate events in the Synoptics. The Marcan order is the basic order followed by both Matthew and Luke. Below follows a list of thirty-one consecutive passages in Mark extending from the beginning of Jesus' ministry to the end of chapter 6. Alongside them are listed the parallel passages as they are found in Matthew and Luke. Note the completely unbroken continuity of order in the Marcan column. Note also the meaning of the symbols 0-0-0 and x-x-x in comment (a) following the list.

	Matthew	Mark	Luke
1. Good News first proclaimed	4:12–17	1:14–15	4:14–15
2. Call of the first disciples	4:18–22	1:16–20	0-0-0
3. In the synagogue of Capernaum	0-0-0	1:21–28	4:31–37
4. Healing of Peter's wife's mother	0-0-0	1:29–31	4:38–39
5. Healings in the evening	0-0-0	1:32–34	4:40–41
6. Departure from Capernaum	0-0-0	1:35–38	4:42–43
7. General preaching and healing in Galilee	4:23–25	1:39	4:44
8. Healing of a leper	8:1–4	1:40–45	5:12–16
9. Healing of a paralytic	9:1–8	2:1–12	5:17–26
10. Call of Levi (Matthew)	9:9–13	2:13–17	5:27–32
11. A question about fasting	9:14–17	2:18–22	5:33–39
12. Controversy on the sabbath	12:1–8	2:23–28	6:1–5
13. Healing of a man with a withered hand	12:9–14	3:1–6	6:6–11
14. Healings among the multitude	12:15–21	3:7–12	6:17–19
15. Appointment of the Twelve	0-0-0	3:13–19[a]	0-0-0
16. Controversy about casting out devils	12:22–37	3:19[b]–30	0-0-0
17. The true brethren of Jesus	12:46–50	3:31–35	0-0-0
18. The Sower	13:1–9	4:1–9	8:4–8
19. Interpretation of the Sower	13:10–23	4:10–20	8:9–15
20. Miscellaneous sayings	0-0-0	4:21–25	8:16–18
21. Tares: the seed growing secretly	13:24–30	4:26–29	x-x-x
22. The mustard seed	13:31–32	4:30–32	0-0-0
23. The parabolic method	13:34–35	4:33–34	x-x-x
24. Stilling of the storm	0-0-0	4:35–41	8:22–25
25. The Gerasene demoniac	0-0-0	5:1–20	8:26–39
26. Jairus' daughter and the woman with an issue of blood	0-0-0	5:21–43	8:40–56
27. Rejection in the synagogue	13:53–58	6:1–6[a]	0-0-0
28. General teaching	0-0-0	6:6[b]	0-0-0
29. The mission of the Twelve	0-0-0	6:7–13	9:1–6[b]
30. Herod's opinion of Jesus and the death of John the Baptist	14:1–12	6:14–29	9:7–9
31. Return of the Twelve and the feeding of the five thousand	14:13–21	6:30–44	9:10–17*

*For the titles and passages of this listing I am indebted to H. F. D. Sparks' *A Synopsis of the Gospels* (Part I, Second Edition, 1970), pp. xvi–xix.

Attention is called to the following:

    a) The list of Marcan passages is completely consecutive. There are no breaks between 1:14–15 and 6:30–34. The open spots indicated by 0-0-0 mean that the book concerned has the same material but in a different order than that in which Mark presents it. The sign x-x-x means that there is no corresponding material in the book concerned.

    b) In the list Matthew conforms to Mark twenty out of thirty-one times; Luke conforms twenty-two times. By "conform" here we mean that the passages in Matthew and Luke stand in the same order of events as the order that is indicated in the Marcan account.

    c) Matthew and Mark agree against Luke; Luke and Mark agree against Matthew. But Matthew and Luke do not agree against Mark. In all disagreements with his order Mark is always supported by one of the others. In 3:13–19[a] and 6:6[b] both Matthew and Luke disagree with Mark, but they do not agree with each other.

    d) In the Synoptics as a whole, all three are in agreement on identity of order in sixty-two passages. Matthew and Mark are in separate agreement in twenty-three instances, and Luke and Mark in ten.

    It is especially considerations like these that have led the majority of New Testament scholars to attribute priority of writing to Mark and dependence of Matthew and Luke upon him.

CHAPTER VIII

JOHN

The last of the four gospels stands in a class by itself. It includes, as we shall note, some material parallel to the Synoptics—but this is not a major aspect of the gospel of John. It is, if we may so put it, a theological treatise in the form of a narrative. It is characterized by simplicity of expression and religious warmth. At the same time, and in spite of its simplicity, the thought of John again and again is so profound that no book in the Bible, with the possible exception of Romans, has more challenged the theological thinker. We approach the fourth gospel therefore in both a devout and thoughtful attitude. Whoever so reads John cannot fail to be enriched in heart and mind.

AUTHOR

Of the four gospels John has the strongest evidence of authorship. This is found in 21:20–24, where we read, "This is the disciple who is bearing witness to these things, and who has written these things, and we know that his testimony is true" (vs. 24). Who is this disciple? It is clearly "the disciple whom Jesus loved, who had lain close to his breast at the supper" (v. 20). But who was "the disciple whom Jesus loved"? There is no direct statement in the gospel that it was John the apostle, the brother of James, the son of Zebedee. The evidence that it was he, however, is very strong and rests on the following passages:

13:23–25   where the disciple whom Jesus loved is identified as lying closest to Jesus at the last supper.
19:25–27   where Jesus, having been crucified, gives his mother into the hands of the beloved disciple.
20:2–10   where Peter and "the other disciple," having been informed by Mary Magdalene, go to the open tomb. The "other disciple" is identified as "the one whom Jesus loved." In this passage he is referred to four times as "the other disciple." (Cf. also 18:15, 16 where Peter and "another disciple" follow Jesus into the court of the high priest.)

64

21:7   where the beloved disciple recognizes Jesus from the boat in
which he and Peter and the other disciples are fishing.

21:20-23   where he is the man about whom Jesus speaks mysteri-
ously in connection with his return.

21:24   where the disciple whom Jesus loved is identified as "the disciple . . . who has written these things."

Further, it is very likely that he who saw the soldiers pierce
Jesus' side with a spear and "has borne witness—his testimony is
true and he knows that he tells the truth—that you also may believe"
is the same as the beloved disciple (19:26, 34, 35). In view of these
various testimonies it would also appear to be clear that the beloved
disciple was one of the Twelve.

The fact that the beloved disciple was one of the Twelve does
not yet establish that he was John, however. For this we must further
consider that according to the Synoptics, Peter, along with James
and John, the sons of Zebedee, formed Jesus' inner circle among
the Twelve (Mark 5:37 [Luke 8:51]; Mark 9:2 [Matt. 17:1; Luke
9:28]; Mark 14:33 [Matt. 26:37]). There is also a very close association between Peter and John (Acts 3:1-11; 4:13; 8:14). James was
killed by Herod (Acts 12:2), leaving Peter and John. It is therefore
extremely significant that in every mention of the beloved disciple
in the gospel of John (except 19:26), Peter is prominently associated
with him. All of these considerations point strongly to John as the
beloved disciple and therefore to him as the author of the fourth
gospel.

John's authorship is further, though indirectly, supported by
the fact that nowhere in the gospel is he referred to by name. The
closest reference to John personally is in 21:2 where Jesus reveals
himself, among others, to "the sons of Zebedee." (In all probability,
however, this chapter was not written by John, as we shall note
below.) In short, John the author, it would appear, was concerned
to keep himself nameless.

The question then arises: Why did John refer to himself as the
disciple whom Jesus loved? If modesty led him to keep himself
nameless, why did he repeatedly make special mention of himself
as "the disciple whom Jesus loved"? Could he not have referred to
himself in another way which would not give the appearance of self-
praise? A look at chapter 21 may shed some light here.

Many scholars do not consider the twenty-first chapter part of
the original gospel, which was fittingly concluded with the last two
verses of chapter 20: "Now Jesus did many other signs in the presence of his disciples, which are not written in this book, but these

are written that you may believe that Jesus is the Christ, the Son of God, and that believing you may have life in his name." The twenty-first chapter would therefore be an appendix added by an editor or editors. In 21:24 the words "we know" speak concerning "his testimony." The "we" would here appear to refer to the editors and the "his" to the testimony of the beloved disciple, that is, to the book as a whole.

In this connection it is interesting to note that the writer refers to the beloved disciple in various ways: "one of his disciples" (13:23); "the disciple" (19:27); "the other disciple" (20:2–10 four times); "this man," "this disciple," "the other disciple" (18:15). It is entirely possible 1) that John in his writing of the gospel used the expression "the other disciple" (or one like it) to refer to himself, 2) that editors introduced the expression "the beloved disciple," but 3) retained here and there John's own self-designation as "the other disciple." The most important verse designating John as the disciple whom Jesus loved is doubtless 13:23: "One of his disciples, whom Jesus loved, was lying close to the breast of Jesus." It is altogether possible that the words "whom Jesus loved" were inserted by an editor and that similar changes or additions were made in other places.

Given the background of these considerations, the following view of the authorship of the gospel seems likely. The fundamental content of the gospel was written by John the apostle. He wrote it on the basis of his knowledge and recollections of the teachings of Jesus. As he grew older he became the most distinguished of the disciples that had accompanied Jesus. There developed around him a group of disciples that may be called "a school"; these were men who knew his thought intimately. Among them were some who combined education and a knowledge of the thought of their times with their Christian faith and the teaching that they had learned from John. One or more of these developed John's original gospel account into the gospel that we now have.

In ancient times there was not the same careful and exclusive view of authorship that we have today. Ecclesiastes was written in the name of Solomon by a man who lived hundreds of years after him. The Psalms are often called the Psalms of David, but he by no means wrote all of them. Moses did not write all of the Pentateuch, better known as the Five Books of Moses. By viewing the writing of John in this light, Johannine authorship is retained while aspects of it are explained that would otherwise be difficult to account for.

The external evidence that John the apostle is the author of the fourth gospel is very strong indeed. The church fathers Justin Martyr, Irenaeus, Tertullian, Origen, and Jerome, along with other witnesses, all testify to it.

DATE OF WRITING

In the nineteenth century and in the earlier part of the twentieth many scholars dated the writing of the gospel of John well into the second century. More conservative estimates placed its writing in the last decade of the first century. These datings, which are late compared with the Synoptics, were based on several suppositions. One was that John was somewhat dependent on the Synoptics and therefore wrote after them. Another was the supposed existence of a connection between the gospel and Gnostic thought* that flourished in the second century. A third was that John's deeper insights grew out of earlier and simpler theological thinking in the church. This development, it was thought, could not have taken place before late in the first or early in the second century.

New Testament studies in the past forty years have considerably altered these views of the dating of John. Papyrus fragments of the New Testament found in Egypt in the 1930s indicate that the gospel of John was known there early in the second century. Its writing (probably in Ephesus, see below) would therefore have been completed sometime before then. In the second place, considerable doubt has arisen that John was dependent on the Synoptics. Similarities between John and the Synoptics may be due to separate and independent but in some respects similar oral traditions. If this is true, John could have been written as early as the Synoptics.

The need for time to permit theological ideas to develop must also not be emphasized too strongly. The Prologue of John is doubtless one of its more profound teachings. We find, however, a very similar statement in Colossians 1:15–20 written by Paul who died in the mid-sixties. John could, therefore, have been written in its final form in the late sixties or early seventies of the first century. It is perhaps wisest at this point in the discussion among scholars not to be dogmatic as to whether this is actually the case.

PLACE OF WRITING

Ephesus in Asia Minor is the city traditionally mentioned as the place where the fourth gospel was written. About A.D. 190 Irenaeus

---

*See section on "Purpose and Background."

wrote, "John the disciple of the Lord, who leaned back on his breast, himself too set forth the gospel while dwelling in Ephesus, the city of Asia" (Eusebius, *Ecclesiastical History*, V:20). According to other traditions John lived there the latter part of his life and was buried there. There is also a tradition of two Johns residing in Ephesus, John the apostle and John the elder. Alongside this there is a tradition of two graves in Ephesus, one for each John.

Over against these testimonies stands a significant silence on the part of Ignatius, bishop of Antioch in Syria about A.D. 115. On his well-known journey to Rome to be martyred by the Roman government, he wrote a number of letters to churches in Asia Minor. One of them was to Ephesus. In it he praises Ephesus for its Christian tradition, refers to Paul's relationship to it, but is entirely silent about John. Since John was the most famous Christian at the time of Ignatius's death, this is difficult to understand.

Whatever its incompleteness, more evidence points to Ephesus as the place of composition of the fourth gospel than to any other city or area. Two other possibilities that are mentioned, however, are Alexandria in Egypt and Antioch in Syria.

JOHN AND THE SYNOPTICS

When we compare John with the Synoptics similarities are not absent. The differences between them, however, are many and they are important.

1. *SIMILARITIES*

In common with the Synoptics John reports several well-known events: the descent of the Spirit on Jesus (1:32–34); the cleansing of the temple (2:13–16); the multiplication of loaves (6:1–13); Jesus' walking on the sea (6:16–21); the anointing of Jesus (12:1–8); and his triumphal entry into Jerusalem (12:12–19). In addition to these are the accounts of the passion and the resurrection. There are also a number of separate passages related to, or similar to, synoptic materials (5:8, 9 [Mark 2:11, 12]; 6:7 [Mark 6:37]; 13:38 [Luke 22:34]; 14:31 [Mark 14:42]; 18:10 [Luke 22:34]). All in all, it is estimated that only about eight percent of John has significantly corresponding material in the Synoptics.

2. *DIFFERENCES*

a) A careful reading of the above passages will show that even the similarities may contain substantial differences. Two examples of this may be noted. In John the cleansing of the temple takes place early in Jesus' ministry; in the Synoptics it takes place at the very end. In John the woman who anoints Jesus is Mary, the sister of Lazarus and Martha; in Matthew and Mark she is not identified, while in Luke she is referred to as a woman of ill repute.

b) The Synoptics, it will be recalled, have a common structure for Jesus' ministry. After his baptism and temptation in the wilderness, and when John the Baptist has been imprisoned, Jesus departs to Galilee (Mark 1:14). Nearly the whole of Jesus' preaching, teaching, and healing ministry takes place in Galilee. He then returns to Judea and immediately conflict arises with the scribes and pharisees. This leads to his arrest, trial, and death. Resurrection appearances are in Galilee (Matthew and Mark) and in Jerusalem (Luke).

In John, Jesus' ministry does not begin *after* John the Baptist has been imprisoned; rather, it is carried on for a while at the same time as the Baptist's. John places Jesus in Galilee only in 2:1–12, 4:43–54, and finally in connection with the feeding of the five thousand and the long discourse on the bread of life in 6:1–7:9. In 4:1–42 Jesus is in Samaria. In John's gospel, by far the larger part of Jesus' ministry takes place in Judea. After the resurrection Jesus appears both in Jerusalem and in Galilee.

c) John refers to three Passovers in the course of Jesus' ministry (2:13ff.; 6:4; 12:1ff.); the Synoptics mention only one Passover, the feast at which Jesus was crucified. According to John, therefore, Jesus' ministry lasted at least two years. In contrast, in the Synoptics Jesus' ministry presumably did not last even two years. It is entirely possible, though, that the Synoptics simply do not mention the other Passovers that took place in the course of the ministry.

d) By far the most important difference between John and the Synoptists lies in the manner in which they present Jesus to the reader. In the Synoptics the direct revelation of Jesus' messianic character is very gradual and restrained. In John it is direct, early, unrestrained, and constant. In the Synoptics, toward the end of his ministry, Jesus asked his disciples, "Who do men say that I am?" In Matthew, Peter gives the fullest answer, "You are the Christ, the Son of the living God" (16:16). Thereupon Matthew reports, ". . . he strictly charged the disciples to tell no one that he was the Christ" (v. 20).

This contrasts remarkably with John. In the very first chapter the Baptist introduces Jesus, saying, "Behold the Lamb of God who takes away the sin of the world" (vv. 29, 36). In the same chapter Philip tells Nathanael, "We have found him of whom Moses in the

law and also the prophets wrote . . ." (v. 45). Nathanael meets Jesus
and exclaims, "Rabbi, you are the Son of God! You are the King
of Israel!" (v. 49). At the well of Sychar in Samaria a woman with
whom Jesus talked said, "I know that Messiah is coming. . . ."
Jesus said to her, "I am he" (4:25, 26). To the Jews he said, "Before
Abraham was, I am" (8:58).

It is not only in such statements that John presents Jesus to the
reader. The whole book, from beginning to end, is a testimony to
Jesus' divine character. He who comes from heaven is above all; he
bears witness to what he has seen and heard (3:31, 32). Everyone
who drinks of earthly water will thirst again, but whoever drinks of
the water that Jesus shall give him will never thirst (4:13, 14). The
Son can only do what he sees the Father doing; the Father loves the
Son and shows him all that he himself is doing (5:19). Jesus is the
light of the world (8:1), and he is from above (8:23). The Father is
in him and he is in the Father (10:38). He is the resurrection and
the life (11:25). This large and continuous testimony climaxes in the
confession of Thomas, who said, "My Lord and my God" (20:28).
Yet it is not only in these texts and passages, but in the whole of the
book—in miracles, discourses, and controversy—that this divine
messianic character is put forward.

This theme is, of course, also found in the Synoptics. Peter
confesses that Jesus is the Christ. Only the Son knows the Father
and only the Son can reveal him (Matt. 11:27). He has the power to
forgive sin, (Mark 2:10). His "but I say to you" (Matt. 5:22, 28, 32,
etc.) manifests an authority that is higher than that of the Old Testament. But it is not the direct, the deliberate, the exclusive theme
that it is in John. Moreover, there are occasions in the Synoptics
when Jesus, having revealed his power or origin, forbids that it be
reported.

e) There is another difference between John and the Synoptics
that works in exactly the opposite direction; that is, Jesus' instruction in the life of Christian obedience. In the Synoptics this aspect
of Jesus' teaching is extremely rich and diverse. The Sermon on the
Mount and the many other teachings with their various instructions
on evangelism, the kingdom parables, the keeping of the law, the
use of the sabbath, the stewardship of money, mutual forgiveness,
hospitality, church discipline, divorce, neighborliness, humility, the
devotional life, and prayer are set forth with unforgettable force and
illustrations that are quite wanting in the gospel of John.

John certainly teaches the Christian life, but it is presented less
concretely and specifically than in the Synoptics. It is set forth as

the demand of love: "If you love me you will keep my commandments" (14:15); "This is my commandment, that you love one another as I have loved you" (15:12). But the practical meaning of this
is not set forth with anything approaching the detail and force of the
Synoptics.

It is clear that no one gospel presents the whole of the rich
truth about the person, the work, and the words of our Lord Jesus
Christ. As the three Synoptists mutually complement and enrich
each other, so do John and the Synoptists together strenthen and fill
out each other's teaching.

PURPOSE AND BACKGROUND

None of the gospels has stated its purpose more clearly than the
gospel according to John:

> Now Jesus did many other signs in the presence of his disciples, which
> are not written in this book; but these are written that you may believe
> that Jesus is the Christ, the Son of God, and that believing you may
> have life in his name (20:30, 31).

This short statement conveys several important ideas. One is that
the gospel is a book of "signs," that is, of demonstrations or evi-
dences about the person and work of Jesus. Many commentators
call chapters 2–12 "the book of signs." The signs that John reports,
however, are only a few of the many that Jesus did (20:30; 21:25).
Second, in reporting them John has a double purpose. The first part
is evangelistic in character. The signs that are reported "are written
that you may believe that Jesus is the Christ," that is, the Messiah,
the Son of God, the fulfillment of the prophecies of the Old Testament. The other part is that "believing you may have life in his
name." As the first half of the double purpose is to bring men to
the new birth (3:5–8), so the second is to nurture them in that faith
to full life in Christ (6:50, 51).

The question we must try to answer is: who are the "you" in
the words "that you may believe" and in "that you may have life
in his name"? This has been a much debated question among
theologians.

Some have said that John was written to make the meaning of
the gospel plain to the Greek world. There were good reasons for
holding this view. John is by far the most theological of the four
gospels. This would make it appeal to the philosophic mind for
which the Greeks were well known. The Prologue with its emphasis

on the Word immediately calls to mind the eternal *logos* (word) of Greek philosophy, which was the basis for order and harmony in the world. Moreover, Greek thinking was dualistic, that is, it believed in two eternal principles neither of which could overcome the other. These were spirit, the source of good, and matter, the source of evil. John would seem to be making Christian use of this basic Greek idea in such contrasts as life and death, above and below, light and darkness, spirit and flesh. Toward the end of the first century a pagan religious movement known as Gnosticism (salvation by knowledge) began to be influential in the Greek world. It was basically dualism in religious dress. Was John's gospel an effort to reach the followers of these views in language that they could understand?

Others have held as strongly that John is a gospel for the Jews. The idea of *logos* in the Prologue could as well be drawn from the Old Testament use of *dabhar*, Hebrew for "word," as from the Greek. It is the central word used in the Old Testament for the communication of God's revelation to the prophets. (An example of its use is the passage "by the *dabhar* of the Lord were the heavens made," Ps. 33:6.) Furthermore, the scene of John is set wholly in Palestine and especially in Jerusalem, and much of the book is devoted to Jesus' controversy with the Jews, a subject that would not be of primary interest to the Greek world. In addition, the Old Testament background is strong throughout. Finally, who were "his own home" and "his own people" (1:11), if not Palestine and the Jews? Thus, it is clear that the case is even stronger for the Jewish purpose and background of the gospel than for the Greek.

During the past twenty-five years this long debate has, at least to a large extent, been decided. This has been done in a remarkable and happy way with a victory for neither side. Between 1947 and 1960 ancient documents were discovered in Palestine that were written about the time of Christ by a Jewish religious group or order known as the Essenes. The place near which they were found is called Qumran, on the Dead Sea, the site of a large monastary of the order. Some of these documents use many words, expressions, and ideas that are characteristic of John, such as "do the truth," "walking in darkness," "sons of error," "sons of light," "light of life." Moreover, the sharp contrasts of above and below, good and evil, flesh and spirit, life and death, light and darkness are found frequently in the Qumran books. But the dualism that is also present in the Qumran scrolls is different from Greek dualism, and very like that in John. In Greek philosophy and in Gnosticism the opposites are equal, each is eternal, and neither can conquer the other. This

is not true of the opposites of the Qumran scrolls. In them the
Creator God of the Old Testament stands supreme over all. He main-
tains the good, will save the righteous, and will destroy all evil. This
John also believed and taught. But he introduced an altogether new
element that neither Greek philosophy, nor Jewish religion, nor Essene theology provided: he presented Christ as the Way, the Truth,
and the Life, the glorious Victor over all the powers of darkness.

It would appear, then, that the men of Qumran developed Jewish religious thought with the aid of Greek ideas. Since the conquests
of Alexander the Great (died 323 B.C.), these ideas had influenced
the ancient world of which Palestine was a crossroad. Greek ideas
had entered Jewish religious thinking, had been modified by it, and
had at the time of Christ found a particular place in Essene thought.
It is altogether possible that John drew ideas from their thought as
they were expressed in the Qumran documents and possibly others
long since lost. By means of them he spoke the gospel to both the
Jews and the Greeks.

THEOLOGY

John's gospel is undoubtedly the most theological of the four. It has
indeed been called "the theological gospel." By this is meant that
its thought is more unified and systematic than that of the Synoptics.
The language is also more symbolic, full of hidden meanings. At the
same time, though, John has been simply written. Thus, it is a favorite book of both learned theologians and simple believers. In this
section we shall discuss four topics in which the theological character of the gospel comes to special expression. They are: 1) the
person of Christ, 2) the new life in Christ, 3) teaching concerning
the Church, and 4) teaching concerning the End. In systematic theology these matters touch on the areas of Christology (doctrine of
Christ), Soteriology (doctrine of salvation), Ecclesiology (doctrine
of the Church), and Eschatology (doctrine of the End), respectively.

1. *CHRISTOLOGY*
The key to the understanding of "The Gospel According to
John" is the Prologue (1:1–18). It states that the Word existed in the
beginning; that the Word was with God and was God; that all things
were created by him; that he is the light and the life of men; that he
became a human being; that the world did not receive him, but that
to those who believed in him he gave power to become the children
of God.

The name that John gave to the Son is "the Word"; in the Greek, *logos*. Of him John says on the one hand that he is distinct from God (he is "with" him), but on the other, that he is very God. This is the mystery of the being of God. The Greek word *logos* can variously mean "thought," "reason," or "order"; it can also be the Greek translation of the Hebrew *dabhar*, which means "word." This normally refers to the spoken word, but when applied to God it means "spoken-word-in-action," as in: God *said* let there *be* light, and there *was* light. The Logos may therefore be described as the God who causes his creative thought to become external created reality. He it was who created the world through his word of power, and gave to it order, harmony, and meaning. He it is who is the light and life of men and of all that lives.

In the section "John and the Synoptics," under *Differences*, the fourth point compares the manner in which John presents Jesus to his readers with the manner in which the Synoptics present him. That material should be regarded as an essential part of the present christological discussion.

2. *THE NEW LIFE IN CHRIST*

One of the richest elements in John's gospel is its teaching concerning life. No book in the New Testament speaks more meaningfully about what true life is than John does. It is the word that gathers together all the benefits of salvation in Christ. The purpose of the writing of the gospel is summed up in the one word "life" in the phrase, "that believing you may have *life* in his name" (20:31).

The roots of the true life of the believer reach deeply into the very life of God. The Father has life in himself, and he has given the Son to have life in himself (5:26). The life of the Son is the light of men (1:4): he who believes in him *has* eternal life; whoever does not obey the Son shall not see life (3:36). This life is given by the Holy Spirit (3:8), who himself is this life, and all who believe in Christ receive it (7:38, 39). The Son gives food that endures to eternal life (6:27), for whoever eats his flesh and drinks his blood has eternal life (6:54). Jesus is the resurrection and the life; he who believes in him, though he die, yet shall he live (11:25). This life is nourished by abiding in Christ (15:17); it glorifies God by bearing much fruit (15:8); this fruit is that we love one another as Christ has loved us (15:9-17).

This language is not found in the Synoptics. Yet it would be a mistake to suppose that therefore the matter represented by these words is not found in Matthew, Mark, and Luke. Rather, it appears in them in the frequently recurring "kingdom of heaven" and "kingdom of God." The expression "enter the kingdom" in Matthew (5:20; 7:21; 18:3; 19:23) and related passages in Mark and Luke would appear to have the same meaning there as receiving life has in John. Indeed, in Matthew's rendering of the parable of the rich young ruler the expressions "enter life" (19:17) and "enter the kingdom of God" (19:23) would appear to have identical meanings.

This life in Christ, like the Synoptic teaching about the kingdom, is a present reality. Eternal life does not begin after death, nor does the reality of the kingdom. Both begin with the decision to follow Christ. To know the only true God and Jesus Christ whom he has sent *is* eternal life, (17:3). Matthew speaks the same thought in his way: the poor in spirit are blessed, for theirs *is* the kingdom of heaven (5:3).

3. *THE CHURCH AND ITS SACRAMENTS*

The question has been raised whether the church and its sacraments are in any way reflected in John. Some students of the gospel feel that it speaks only of the individual believer's relationship to Jesus. It is true that there is no specific reference in John to the church or its government (as in Matt. 18); nor is there any reference in it by name or ritual act to the sacraments of the church as in the other gospels. But does silence about these matters mean lack of awareness or appreciation of them? There are, in fact, a number of references in the gospel of John that are difficult to understand apart from the author's direct involvement in the life of the church.

a) The church

The passage, "I do not pray for these only but also for those who are to believe in me through their word, that they may all be one (17:20, 21ᵃ [cf. also 21ᵇ, 22, 23]) speaks a language that the church understands. It has taken these words to refer to its missionary outreach and its unity. Missionary concern is also found in "the fields that are already white for the harvest" (4:35), and it is further reflected in "he who receives anyone whom I send receives me" (13:20). A similar authority to speak in Jesus' name is presented in his well-known words, "If you forgive the sins of any, they are forgiven; if you retain the sins of any they are retained" (20:23). It would appear, then, that the disciples here represent the whole of the subsequent church that continues to act on this authority.

Further, there are the rather massive examples of the church as a fellowshipping body in the figures of the vine and the branches (ch. 15), the shepherd, the sheep, and the sheepfold (ch. 10), and in Jesus' instruction to Peter to feed his sheep and his lambs (ch. 21). There is here more than a mere individual following of Jesus—there are clear indications of the closest fellowship between Christ and his people and of the exercise of his authority among them. There can be no doubt that from the earliest times the church as a fellowship as well as believers individually has drawn much instruction and comfort from these words.

b) The sacraments

Similar considerations would seem to apply to the sacraments. Was Jesus really silent about them? Did he perhaps speak about them without using the accustomed words? It is difficult not to think of baptism when in 3:5 we read, "unless one is born of water and the Spirit, he cannot enter the kingdom of God." The footwashing in 13:11 may not point to baptism in the first order, but rather to the need for daily pardon for sin; but it is significant that when Peter wants more than his feet washed Jesus says, "He who has bathed does not need to wash, except for his feet, but he is clean all over . . ." (v. 10). Does not the "bathing" and the being "clean all over" refer in their deeper meaning to the sacramental act of baptism with its renewal of the whole man?

The Lord's Supper finds a strong symbol in the great sixth chapter of John, which speaks of Jesus as the bread of life. Verse 53 is notable: ". . . unless you eat the flesh of the Son of man and drink his blood, you have no life in you." In 15:1–11 there is no specific reference either to bread or to wine; rather the illustration for intimate union and fellowship is a vine on which grapes grow from which wine is made.

Finally, there is the remarkable report in 19:34, "But one of the soldiers pierced his side with a spear and at once there came out blood and water." Here the blood celebrated by the wine of communion and cleansing water celebrated in baptism both flow from the body of the crucified one.

4. TEACHING CONCERNING THE END

John's doctrine concerning the End is best understood when it is compared with the teaching about the End in the Synoptics. There the doctrine about "the last things" builds on Old Testament teaching. In that view history continues in a straight line to its very end. Then comes the judgment, and with the judgment the End. A favorite Old Testament designation for it is "the Day of the Lord."

The Synoptics continue this view of the End, but they enrich it by presenting Jesus as the final Deliverer and Judge. They make clear that the judgment of Christ closes off the present Age and introduces the Age to come. Mark 13, Matthew 24, 25, and Luke 21:5–36 set forth the synoptic view of the End, each in its own way.

In John the synoptic view of the End is not ignored or denied, but it differs from his main view of the End. For John the End is also and very importantly a *present* reality. In John the End is here; the End is now. The new Age is a present reality: "Truly, truly, I say to you, he who hears my word and believes him who sent me, has eternal life; he does not come into judgment, but has passed from death to life" (5:24). The decisive moment is now. The judgment is today:

> Truly, truly, I say to you, the hour is coming *and now is*, when the dead will hear the voice of the Son of God, and those who hear will live. For as the Father has life in himself, so he has granted the Son also to have life in himself, and has given him authority to execute judgment, because he is the Son of man (5:25–27).

Here "the dead" are those who are spiritually dead. The true hearing of the voice of the Son of God is the response of faith to the gospel. Eternal life is the life of the new Age projecting itself into the life of the present Age. "And this is eternal life, that they know thee, the only true God, and Jesus Christ whom thou hast sent" (17:23).

At the same time, however, John retains the synoptic teaching of a final end of history (5:28, 29). The spiritual resurrection that believers enjoy now shall be completed in the physical resurrection at the end of time. He who eats the flesh and drinks the blood of Christ *has eternal life*, and he will raise him up *at the last day* (6:54). John emphasizes the End that is now without ignoring the End that is still future. The Synoptists present the End as future without ignoring its reality here and now.

STRUCTURE

When we speak of the structure of John we have a somewhat different matter in mind than when we speak of the structure of the Synoptics. The structure that we discovered in them is based on a geographic order, namely, the areas in which Jesus successively performed his ministry. In John a deeper kind of structure is discernible. It refers not so much to the order in which parts of the book *follow* each other, but to the manner in which parts of the book are *related* to each other.

We call attention to the following: 1) the relationship of chapter 1 to the rest of the book; 2) the relationship of event to discourse in chapters 2–12; 3) the plan of chapters 13–17; and 4) the relationship of chapters 18–21 to the rest of the book.

1. THE RELATIONSHIP OF CHAPTER 1 TO THE REST OF THE BOOK

The Prologue, vv. 1–18, sets Christ forth as the incarnate Word, the Creator of all that is, one who was with God, yet is very God, who became man. John's witness, vv. 19–36, introduces Christ in his servant form: "Behold the Lamb of God who takes away the sin of the world." These two themes of deity and servanthood through which Christ reconciles man to God control the whole of the book. Verses 37–51 show the beginning of the disciple group which became the human base from which Jesus performed his ministry.

2. THE RELATIONSHIP OF EVENT TO DISCOURSE IN THE PUBLIC MINISTRY (chapters 2–12)

In the Synoptics, especially in Matthew, events and discourses are in varying degrees related to each other. In John event and discourse are inseparable. The event is the foundation of the oral teaching that follow it. The speaking is an interpretation that exposes the deeper meaning of the event. We may call chapters 2–12 interpreted-event-material.

The cleansing of the temple (2:13–22), the visit of Nicodemus (3:1ff.), the feeding of the five thousand (6:5ff.), the healing of the man born blind (9:1ff.), the raising of Lazarus from the dead (ch. 11), and the request of the Greeks to see Jesus (12:20ff.)—all these events lead to or are preceded by teaching that is directly related to the event. This relationship is basic in the structure of John in chapters 2 to 12. Since a number of the events are miraculous acts of Jesus called "signs," the whole of chapters 2 to 12 is often called "the Book of Signs."

It is true that John does not follow this pattern 100 percent. Sometimes, as in the changing of water into wine at Cana (2:1–11), or in the healing of the official's son (4:46–54), there is no oral interpretation. The event has its own meaning. But it is instructive to note that both of them are called signs (2:11; 4:54). John expected the believer who saw these signs to see also the manifestation of Jesus' glory in them.

The word "discourse" in the sense in which we use it here must be correctly understood. It can have the meaning of uninterrupted speech such as a lecture or a sermon, but it can also mean conversation or dialogue. John presents both kinds of discourse in chapters 2 to 12. That is, in 5:19–47 we find only uninterrupted speech, in 10:1–18 there is one interruption, and in 6:25–65 Jesus teaches with a number of short interruptions. All the remaining speaking by Jesus in chapters 2–12 is of a dialogue character.

The paragraph on Symbolism (see characteristics below) sheds further light on the relationship between event and discourse in John.

3. THE PLAN OF THE PRIVATE INSTRUCTION
   (chapters 13 to 17)

In all four gospels we may distinguish between the public teaching of Jesus and his private instruction of the disciples. In the Synoptics both run alongside each other, although the private instruction becomes more marked as Jesus approaches the Passion. In John the two are separated completely. Chapters 2 to 12 report Jesus' public ministry, while 13–17 report his private instruction. These latter chapters are generally called the Farewell Discourses. With the exception of chapter 13 the private instruction appears almost entirely in uninterrupted form. There are very brief interruptions by the disciples in 14:5, 8, 22 and in 16:17, 18, 29, but these serve only to give Jesus opportunity to make his meaning clearer.

The private teaching appears to serve two purposes:

a) It presents in a Johannine way a number of teachings also found in the private instruction in the Synoptics. A few examples must suffice 13:20 (Mark 9:37); 13:36–38 (Mark 14:26–31); 15:13 (Mark 10:45); 16:7–11 (Mark 13:11); and 16:23, 24 (Mark 11:24). (See parallels in the other Synoptists).

b) The private instruction seeks to develop and enrich some of the major teachings of the Book of Signs. For example, the theme of life, one of the teachings in chapters 2–12 (where the word "life" appears some fifty times), is further enriched in chapters 13–17 by the teaching concerning love. In these five chapters alone the word is mentioned some twenty-five times. Here the teaching concerning life is importantly expressed as mutual indwelling of Father and Son (14:10, 11), which carries over to mutual indwelling of Christ and believers (15:4, 5). This life, then, is expressed in love. The Son loves the Father (14:31); the Father loves the Son (15:9, 17:23). This mutual life and love becomes part of the life of the disciples (15:9,

10, 12; 17:23; 14:19–21). A similar pattern develops with the themes of fellowship and obedience.

The high priestly prayer (chapter 17) is a moving and beautiful conclusion to the entire public and private ministry of Jesus. In it Jesus asks his Father to actualize in the lives of the disciples, present and future, some of his major teachings relating to glory, eternal life, his sending of the disciples, and the unity of the disciples.

4. THE RELATION BETWEEN CHAPTERS 1–17 AND 18–21

The connection between these two sections in John is a very close one. In John the reader is prepared from the very first chapter to face the suffering and death of Jesus. Moreover, this preparation continues throughout the following sixteen chapters. In the Synoptics there is also such a preparation, but it is much less regular. It is more referred to on particular occasions than a constant theme in the books. These occasions occur almost entirely toward the end of Jesus' ministry. Their notable beginning is Mark 8:31 (see Matt. 16:21 and Luke 9:22).

In John, on the other hand, the Baptist in the very first chapter presents Jesus to Israel with the words: "Behold the Lamb of God . . ." (vv. 29, 36). The designation of Jesus as "lamb" unmistakably relates him to sacrifice. At the beginning of his ministry Jesus established his authority to cleanse the temple with a prediction of his death (2:19). The Son of man must be lifted up (3:14); his flesh is life for the world (6:51); he lays down his life for the sheep (10:11). The high priest judges that it is necessary for one man to die for the people (11:50). A question of Greeks at the Passover elicits from Jesus a prediction of the saving power of his death (12:20–28). In chapters 13–17, Jesus speaks of his death as a glorification and a going to the Father. Because of this intimate relationship between Jesus' ministry and his suffering, the expectation of and preparation for Jesus' death comes to the reader earlier in John than in the Synoptics. Suffering, death, and resurrection in chapters 18–21 relate the fulfillment of this preparation.

CHARACTERISTICS

The gospel of John is indeed a gospel in the sense in which that form of writing was defined in the introductory chapter. It is an account of the ministry of Jesus, and as such it belongs to the family of writings called gospels. It is not, however, a synoptic gospel. It lacks altogether the similarity of content and plan that characterizes the first three gospels. The relationship of John to the Synoptics has been discussed earlier in this chapter, and in the section on the theology of John we have noted its differences with the Synoptics. In this section we shall call attention to other characteristic features of the fourth gospel.

1. SYMBOLISM

A marked feature in the writing of John is the use of symbols. It is an essential element in the composition of the gospel. A symbol may be defined as a thing or an idea that, because of associations connected with it, points to something else. A sword may point to war, sugar to sweetness, light to knowledge, darkness to ignorance, blood to loss of life. Examples of symbolic language in John are: above and below, spirit and flesh, life and death, light and darkness, shepherd and sheep, flock and wolf, vine and branches, gardener and fruit—all simple figures that are drawn from everyday experience. Yet they clearly point to realities that touch the deepest things in our relationship to each other and to God. Things that are temporal and passing away are used to point to things that are eternal.

2. MYSTICISM

Closely related to symbolism is mysticism, which represents a kind of religious understanding that is characteristic of the fourth gospel. Mysticism has to do with that aspect of the religion that the mind cannot clearly grasp and define in words. It is a feeling, a being aware of spiritual realities that cannot be expressed. In Romans 8:22, 23 Paul writes that both creation and believers "groan" as they await the redemption of the children of God. In verse 26 he says that the Spirit intercedes for us with "sighs too deep for words." In Jesus' words (John 3:7, 8), "Do not marvel . . . the wind blows where it wills . . . so it is with everyone who is born of the Spirit," we have a typical Johannine example of such writing.

Mystical literature in the Bible must always be read carefully. Biblical mysticism is rich and illuminating; it is never rootless or lawless. It is always grounded in the facts and realities of the Christian faith. Here especially it is necessary to remember the rule that the Bible is its own best interpreter.

3. CONTROVERSY

In the gospel of John, Jesus is continually engaged in controversy—as he is in the Synoptics. There is, however, a remarkable

difference between the controversy recorded in the Synoptics and
that reported in John. In the Synoptics, Jesus' controversy is with
the Jewish leadership: the pharisees, the scribes, and the sadducees.
In John, Jesus' controversy appears, at least on the surface, to be
with the entire Jewish community. Throughout the gospel he is in
confrontation with "the Jews." At the same time, however, it cannot
be denied that, as in Mark 12:57, "the common people heard him
gladly." Crowds followed Jesus, heard him, and sought his healing.
The resurrection of Lazarus especially strengthened Jesus' popularity with the people: ". . . the chief priests planned to put Lazarus
also to death, because on account of him many of the Jews were
going away and believing in him" (12:10, 11). But already before the
raising of Lazarus Jesus had a popular following—as is evident from
many passages (2:23, 26; 4:1; 6:2, 5; 7:31; 8:30; 10:40–42). How
must we then explain the hostility of "the Jews" to Jesus as reported
in John, while at the same time acknowledging that Jesus was broadly
accepted by the Jewish community?

It would appear that the expression "the Jews" very often
means the Jewish leadership rather than the Jewish people or the
local Jewish community. This at least is strongly suggested by passages that indication authoritative action by the Jewish leadership
(1:19; 5:16; 7:13; 9:22; 11:8; 18:31; 19:7, 12). Why, then, the expression "the Jews"? It has been suggested that at the time when John
wrote, the conflict between the Church (i.e., the Christian community) and the Synagogue (i.e., the Jewish community) had become very sharp. John may have read this situation into the time of
Jesus' ministry. This understanding, however, would require a dating
of John rather late in the century, and we have already seen that
recent Johannine scholarship inclines at least in part to an earlier
dating than has been customary. It would appear that until more
light is shed on this problem we have to let it rest with the judgment
that, on the whole, John seems to show a more critical attitude to
the Jewish community than the Synoptists do.

4. THE "ADULTERESS PASSAGE" (7:53– 8:11)

The most ancient manuscripts do not contain the account recorded in 7:53–8:11, which is recorded in many versions of the
Bible. In the opinion of textual critical scholars it represents an oral
tradition in the Church that copyists included in later manuscripts.
Different copyists inserted it in different places in John's gospel.
The most common one is between 7:52 and 8:12. It has also been
placed at the end of Luke 21. In the King James Bible it is printed

as a normal part of the text. The Revised Standard Version (1946), took it out of the text and printed it as a footnote. The New English Bible (1961) prints the passage at the end of the gospel under the heading, "An incident in the temple."

5. *THE EPILOGUE*

As mentioned previously, many New Testament scholars believe that chapter 21 is not a part of the gospel as originally written. The chief reason for this view is the last paragraph of chapter 20:

> Now Jesus did many other signs in the presence of the disciples, which are not written in this book; but these are written that you may believe that Jesus is the Christ, the Son of God, and that believing you may have life in his name (vv. 30, 31).

This is regarded as the original conclusion of the gospel. The reference to "signs," the emphasis on "belief" and "believing," and the purpose of finding "life" by means of his "name" sum up the central teachings of the book. If chapter 21 belonged to the gospel as originally written, then 20:30, 31 would most naturally have been placed at its end as the conclusion of "this book." As it is, 21:25 constitutes a conclusion that in its first part bears considerable similarity to the first half of the final paragraph of chapter 20: "But there are many other things which Jesus did; were every one of them to be written. . . ."

Scholars who believe in the supplementary character of chapter twenty-one are divided between those who believe that John himself wrote the epilogue and those who hold that an editor wrote it. Some hold that chapter 21 was written to show the restoration of Peter after his denial. Others point to differences in style and vocabulary between chapter 21 and the preceding twenty chapters of the gospel to prove that it was written by someone other than John.

It is extremely difficult to judge how another person should have structured what he wrote. This is particularly true of literature that stands many centuries removed from our time. When Paul wrote to the Philippians he began chapter 3 with "Finally, my brethren, rejoice in the Lord . . . ," followed in the next chapter by "Finally, brethren, whatever is true . . ." (4:8). Authors are not always as logical as the analysts of their writings. There are no manuscripts of the fourth gospel, however ancient, in which chapter 21 is missing. The arguments for the supplementary character of chapter 21 are not without value, but they are not conclusive. Until more evidence is adduced to show otherwise, the better working assumption is that the last chapter of John is an integral part of the gospel.

CHAPTER IX

THE ROMAN WORLD

As it was necessary to have some knowledge of the Palestine of Jesus' day to understand the gospels, so it is necessary to have some knowledge of the Roman empire to understand the Acts of the Apostles. The entire history described in the gospels took place in one small country; the history of Acts unfolded in the far larger and more varied area of the greatest empire of antiquity. Although the first twelve chapters of the book confine their action to Palestine, the larger second portion of the book moves from Antioch in Syria through Asia Minor, Palestine, Greece, and back again, and ends in Rome—the center of the then known world. Therefore, we should briefly sketch the main outline of the empire.

HISTORY

About 750 B.C. a man named Romulus founded a village on the banks of the river Tiber in western Italy. Out of it grew the city of Rome, named after its founder. Its people were agressive, expanding the village into a city and pressing its influence and power to the north, to the east, and to the south of the long peninsula. By 270 B.C. Rome was master of Italy. Seventy years later she conquered her great North African rival, Carthage. In due course Spain in the west and Gaul (France) to the north fell into her hands. At the time of Christ all the lands lying around the eastern end of the Mediterranean had also acknowledged her authority. By the end of the first century A.D. Rome governed the vast area that stretched 3,000 miles southeastward from Britain to the Euphrates River, 1,200 miles northward from the western Sahara to the North Sea, and 1,400 miles northward from Egypt to the southern shore of the Black Sea. The empire was bounded on the west by the Atlantic Ocean, on the south by the Sahara Desert, on the north by the Rhine and Danube rivers and the Black Sea, and on the east by the Euphrates River. The most important of these boundaries were the Rhine and the Danube rivers, for east of the former and north of the latter lived many German tribes eager to enter the empire. The major function of the Roman legions was to guard this riverine line of some 1,800 miles.

The church that entered upon her life at Pentecost, therefore, was born in the context of a great empire. But more than that, in the first century A.D. Rome attained her richest and maturest development. In the second century a decline set in that gradually undermined Roman power. In 406 the Germanic tribes broke through the Rhine River barrier, and in 476 the Roman empire in the West came to an end. The eastern section of the empire with its capital at Constantinople continued until 1453, in which year it fell to the Muslims.

PEOPLES AND COMMUNICATIONS

It is estimated that at the beginning of the Christian era the population of the Roman empire was approximately 55,000,000. These were spread among numerous peoples, tribes, and nations. The unity of the empire was chiefly political and economic. Socially, religiously, linguistically, and culturally a more diverse civilization can hardly be imagined. In relation to its many peoples the imperial government was chiefly concerned with three major interests: the regular payment of taxes, a steady supply of recruits for the army, and the acknowledgment of Roman authority. For the rest, it allowed each tribal or national unit to live essentially its own life. Apart from Rome, the great cultural centers were in the east: Alexandria in Egypt, Antioch in Syria, Ephesus in Asia Minor, and Athens in Greece. With the exception of Rome, Italy, Spain, and the whole of Gaul and Britain in the West had no cities comparable to these great urban centers in the East.

To maintain the unity and to enforce the laws in so extensive an area, good communication throughout the empire was a necessity. In the absence of modern motor-driven vehicles and long-distance communication, everything depended on efficient road and ship travel. The Romans provided both. They mastered the art of road building to such an extent that substantial sections of Roman roads survive to this day. On these roads the armies marched, and on them and on the sea and river waterways commerce was conducted and mail and travelers were carried.

Today the Mediterranean Sea is a body of water washing the shores of some fifteen independent countries that surround it. In Roman times it bore quite a different character. Then it was a large inland lake bounded on all sides by the shores of one great power, the Roman empire, and it was governed by one central authority. Moreover, ships could sail through the Straits of Gibralter and travel northward along the coasts of Portugal, Spain, France, the Low Countries and Britain, and the far western and northwestern outposts of the empire. After the break-up of the western empire Europe did not again enjoy such efficient travel and transport services until the nineteenth century.

GOVERNMENT

At the head of this great civilization and great economic, political, and military power stood the emperor. Augustus, adopted son of Julius Caesar, had secured the imperial office in 27 B.C. He restored the Roman Senate to the prestige but not to the power that it had lost some 100 years earlier. He held in his own hand all actual political, military, and financial power. His empire consisted of fifty provinces, each with a governor who was appointed by either the emperor or the Senate; but in either case, the governor was accountable to the emperor. Governors appointed by the Senate were called proconsuls, while those appointed by the emperor were called prefects in the more important provinces and procurators in the less important ones. Order was maintained through the army of which the legion was the basic unit. It consisted of 6,000 men divided into ten cohorts of 600 men each. The cohort was commanded by a tribune, which in turn consisted of six centuries or companies of 100 men commanded by a centurion.

Luke is noted for the careful and specific manner in which he uses such technical terms. For example, he tells us that Sergius Paulus was proconsul of Cyprus (Acts 13:7), and Gallio was proconsul of Achaia (18:12); Cornelius was a centurion who belonged to the Italian Cohort (10:1), while Julius was a centurion in the Augustan Cohort (27:1).

Acts takes us to no less than eight of the eastern provinces: Syria, Cilicia, Judea, Galatia, Asia, Macedonia, Achaia, and Cyprus. Of these Syria was from the Roman point of view perhaps the most important. It was heavily invested militarily because it was a frontier province facing the always hostile Persians. Antioch, its capital city, was regarded, after Alexandria, as the third most influential city in the empire. In Asia (Minor), Ephesus was the capital, and in Macedonia the capital was Thessalonica. Achaia was the name given to ancient Greece (with the exception of Athens, which was a free city with its own government); its capital was Corinth.

Judea with its heavily guarded capital, Jerusalem, was an ever po-
tentially explosive area, for the Jews endured impatiently the yoke
of Roman control. Cilicia was Paul's native country and Tarsus was
its capital. Cyprus was an island province.

Italy was not numbered among the provinces, for it was the
mother country. All other parts of the empire had either been conquered militarily or had been gained by peaceful annexation. All
freemen living in Italy were Roman citizens. In the first century
A.D. citizenship had been extended outside of Italy, but always spar-
ingly and selectively. To be a Roman citizen in the provinces was a
privilege enjoyed by few. It placed its possessor under special pro-
tection of the Roman authorities, forbade beating without trial, and
in litigation gave the right of appeal to the emperor. Paul used these
rights on several dramatic occasions.

THE GREEK INFLUENCE

The civilization of the Roman empire is often referred to as Greco-
Roman rather than as simply Roman. Through the conquests of
Alexander in the fourth century B.C. Greek culture had been extended far to the east and, before that, through colonization far to
the west. When the countries lying east of Italy came under Roman
authority, the intellectual dominance of the Greek mind did not
cease. Greece became the teacher of Rome. The military conquest
of Greece by Rome was followed by the intellectual conquest of
Rome by Greece.

The chief instrument of this conquest was the Greek language,
the medium of education and communication from the Euphrates
westward to Italy and beyond. Its significance in the area of religion
alone can be judged from the fact that the Old Testament had been
translated into Greek already in 250 B.C. in what is called the Septuagint. The entire New Testament was written in Greek. As late as
A.D. 180 Irenaeus, bishop of Lyons in Gaul (France), wrote his great
work *Against Heresies* in Greek. Tertullian, writing in North Africa
from 185 to 220, was the first theologian to write in Latin. As a
result the Gentile mind to which Paul addressed himself in the second part of Acts and in his letters was far more under the influence
of Greek religious and philosophical ideas than under Roman
influence.

THE JEWISH DISPERSION

The Jewish population in the empire outside of Judea was considerably greater than that within it. Over the centuries, commerce and

deportations resulting from war had dispersed Jews throughout the length and breadth of the empire. For millions of Jews, Palestine had religious and historic significance, but their homes, their proper native lands, were in Europe, Asia Minor, Africa, and Mesopotamia. It is estimated that in the first century A.D. two and a half million Jews lived in Palestine proper. Outside of Palestine a million were living in Mesopotamia, another million in Alexandria, and still another million in Asia Minor. Smaller concentrations were found in numerous other localities in the empire. In Italy alone there were a hundred thousand Jews. The Jewish philosopher Philo (died c A.D. 45), himself a resident of Alexandria, wrote that the Jews sought out the prosperous centers of the empire. Their wide spread is attested by the list of nations cited in Acts 2 from which Jews had come to visit Jerusalem.

In the dispersion the Jews remained Jews. They might be called "Hellenist" Jews (Acts 6:1, 9:39) because of their exposure to Greek influences, but they retained their Jewish identity. This was in no small part due to the fact that where the Jews went the synagogue followed them. The Jew and his religion were never separated. In all Paul's travels, whether in Asia Minor or in Macedonia or in Greece, his first concern was to visit and preach in the synagogues. It can be said that the Dispersion, and more particularly the synagogue in the Dispersion, was the starting point for the proclamation of the gospel in Europe and in Asia.

RELIGION

When the spread of Christianity into the empire began, shortly after Pentecost, it found a religiously troubled and groping world. Roman religion was formal and cold. It spoke to patriotic feeling but not to the religious needs of the hearts of men. Its major concern was the security, welfare, and prosperity of the state. Sin, guilt, repentance, forgiveness, communion, prayer, comfort, and praise were not the dimensions in which the gods of Rome moved. Even the disciplined Roman mind was searching for deeper and richer values in religion.

The religion of the peoples in the provinces was varied. Greek philosophy was not without religious significance, but it was too intellectual for the masses. Even for the educated, it rested on human insight and was therefore without ultimate authority. It could not speak the final word of reconciliation and pardon. It did not disclose God to the hearts of men.

The form of religion followed by most was therefore the religion that was traditional in a given area. Temples and religious rites were in evidence everywhere. Some religions spread beyond the areas of their origin and became influential in the empire. Chief of these was the religion of Mithras, a Persian deity of war and light who was identified with Sol Invictus, the unconquerable sun. Mithraism entered the Roman empire in the first century B.C., was very strong by 250, and disappeared about 400. It was popular in the army, especially along the frontiers, and it followed the trade routes and was therefore prominent in the various ports of the empire. It was well represented in Rome, and the emperors encouraged it. In a society corrupt beyond description, it upheld the victory of light over darkness.

Christianity therefore entered the empire as one religion among many. The religions that spread were those that had a message for the hearts of men. The peoples of the empire had open ears for a faith that would give moral and spiritual stability in a morally and spiritually unstable world. Their growth was aided by the fact that the Roman government took a neutral position with respect to religions in the empire. So long as they did not interfere with the established state religion, they were regarded as *religio licita*—lawful religion.

THE FULLNESS OF TIME

In Galatians 4:4 Paul writes, "But when the time had fully come, God sent forth his Son." In its understanding of these words the church has always emphasized the preparation for the coming of the gospel in the Roman empire as an aspect of that "fullness of time." Under the unconscious auspices of the greatest of Rome's emperors, Jesus' parents-to-be made their way to Bethlehem where Mary brought forth her first-born son. The unity of the empire, the prevalence of the Greek language, the convenience and safety of travel, the early neutrality of the government in its relationship to Christianity, the universal sense of need for a revival of religion, the widespread dispersion of the Jews throughout the empire—all these factors combined to give the gospel a powerful send-off in its quest for the loyalties of men and women. More than any other book in the New Testament, the Acts of the Apostles illustrates these providential factors in the history of the church during the first thirty years of its life.

CHAPTER X

THE ACTS OF THE APOSTLES

The Acts of the Apostles concludes the historical section of the New Testament. It carries the record up to the year sixty when Paul arrived in Rome. The fifty years between that event and the second decade of the next century are, so far as church history is concerned, virtually a blank. Except for the martyrdoms of Peter and Paul, and the persecution of the Christians under Nero and Domitian, there is little or no record of the course of church history during this period. A distinguished church historian writes, "though some gleanings can be recovered from this period, the forty years from 70 to 110 remain one of the obscurest portions of church history."

When at the end of these silent decades the character of the church can again be seen, it is evident that extensive changes had taken place. Practices and views with respect to church government, sacraments, liturgy, and doctrine had entered the church that were not present in the last years of Paul and Peter. It is therefore all the more to be appreciated that we possess the record that we have in Acts. It should be used to the fullest extent to understand both the spiritual and historical foundations of the church.

RELATIONSHIP OF ACTS TO LUKE

Luke and Acts are often referred to as one book called Luke-Acts. There are several reasons for this. Both books were written by the same author and were dedicated to the same person. A clear continuity of purpose is evident in the very first words of the dedication in Acts: "In the first book, O Theophilus, I have dealt with all that Jesus began to do and teach. . . ." Luke therefore reports the work that Jesus did on earth, and Acts reports what he continued to do and teach from heaven through the Holy Spirit. It must be observed, however, that the writer refers to the gospel of Luke as "the first book" (or "the former treatise" or "the former narrative," as the translations variously put it). This reference distinguishes it sharply therefore from Acts, the second book. Another difference is that, while the central figure in Luke is Jesus, the central figures in Acts are Peter and Paul. Also, always powerfully in evidence in Acts is the work of the Holy Spirit: Pentecost both begins and dominates the book. Finally, the historical subject matter is altogether different in the two books.

The relationship between Luke and Acts must further be seen in the light of the relationship between the first five books of the New Testament to each other. Matthew, Mark, and Luke are obviously a synoptic group. John stands quite by itself, even though, like the Synoptics, it tells about the earthly ministry of Jesus. The early church, in placing the five books in the canon, quite wisely grouped the three Synoptics and John together as having the ministry, death, and resurrection of Jesus in common. After them it placed Acts as continuing the earthly history of the redemption that the risen Lord had wrought. If it had placed Acts after Luke it would have separated John from the other accounts of Jesus' ministry. If it had united Luke to Acts after John it would have broken up the synoptic group.

Acts is therefore a natural sequence to the four gospels as a whole and to Luke in particular. In the gospels the resurrection of Christ stands immediately related to the crucifixion as victory over death and the grave. In Acts the risen Lord stands immediately related to his ascension and the coming of the Holy Spirit. Whether therefore one speaks of Luke *and* Acts or of Luke-Acts, he is dealing in any case with two distinctive literary units. These are self-contained, on the one hand, and very intimately related, on the other.*

STRUCTURE AND CONTENT

The writers who produced the Bible wrote books—but they did not write them in chapters. Rather, the books were long undivided accounts, broken only here and there by a shorter line to indicate the beginning of a new paragraph. The Bible was not "chapterized" until about 1200. It was not always well done, with the result that chapters often divided matters that belong together. Few books are more obvious in this regard than Acts.

Like Matthew, Acts as a book was carefully planned. This is not, however, clear on the surface; it requires careful reading to

*The question of the authorship of Acts is, for the limited purpose of this book, adequately discussed in the chapter on the gospel of Luke.

distinguish the parts. But the divisions are definitely there. As we shall see, the plan of Acts is very closely related to its purpose and its message. In this section we shall try to understand the structure of the book by indicating and briefly describing its main divisions and their content.

It is very clear from Acts itself that Luke carefully selected the matters that he reported. After chapter twelve we hear no more about Peter. The work of Paul that Acts reports is obviously only a small part of his work as missionary. We hear a word or two about John, a longer reference to James, and nothing at all is said about the other apostles.

The first two chapters are basic to the book as a whole and to every part of it. Chapter 1 lays down the program that is to be carried out, chapter 2 reveals the power by which the program will be executed, and from chapter 3 on Luke relates how the gospel was preached and the church established in the power of the Spirit. He does this in two broad stages, separated by a transition. The first is the spread of the gospel among the Jews, chapters 3–9:31; the second is the spread among the Gentiles, chapters 13–28. The transition covers chapters 9:32–12:25. Each stage has a central figure, Peter in the former, Paul in the latter. The distinction between chapters 3–9:31 and 13–28 as having a Jewish and a Gentile reference respectively must not be taken too literally. There are important Gentile references in the former and reports about the preaching of the gospel to the Jews in the latter. Nevertheless, the general distinction is clear and valid. The structure of the book may therefore be outlined as follows:

I. **Task and Empowerment** (1:1–2:47)
II. **The Church Among the Jews** (Peter)
    A. The Gospel in Jerusalem (3:1–5:42)
    B. The Spread in Judea, Samaria, Galilee and Damascus (6:1–9:31)
III. **Transition to Gentile Mission** (9:32–12:35)
IV. **The Church Among the Gentiles** (Paul)
    A. The Spread into Asia Minor (13:1–16:5)
    B. Advance into Europe (16:6–19:20)
    C. Climax: the Gospel to Rome (19:21–28:31)

Of the seven sections into which Acts is divided only the first two and the fourth end at the close of a chapter. Each is characterized by an appropriate summarizing statement. A brief statement of the contents of each section now follows.

I. *TASK AND EMPOWERMENT* (1:1– 2:47)

Jesus instructs the apostles to wait in Jerusalem for the coming of the Holy Spirit (1:4, 5). When the Holy Spirit has empowered them, they will be his witnesses in Jerusalem, Judea, Samaria, and to the end of the earth (v. 8). This instruction is at the same time the theme of the entire book: the spread of the gospel in the power of the Holy Spirit. Thereupon Jesus ascends to heaven and the disciples return to Jerusalem to await the fulfillment of the promise.

Chapter 2 reports the mighty event of the coming of the Spirit. The gift of the Spirit is the church's empowerment to carry out the command to preach the gospel worldwide. Pentecost is the birthday of the church (2:1–13); on that day 3,000 believed and thereby became the first church community of the New Testament. The summary statement of the section is:

> And the Lord added to their number day by day those who were being saved (2:47[b]).

II. *THE CHURCH AMONG THE JEWS*

A. The Gospel in Jerusalem (3:1– 5:42)

These three chapters form a unit of some eleven incidents, each one leading into the next in a wholly natural way. Peter and John go to the temple for prayer where a lame man appeals to them for a gift and is healed of his lameness (3:1–10). Amazed, the people run together and Peter preaches the gospel to them. This annoys the Sadducees who cause Peter and John to be arrested. The next day they are called to account and Peter preaches to the entire council (4:1–12). Having been warned and threatened, they rejoin their friends who praise God and unite in prayer. So intimate is the fellowship of the believers that they help each other with their gifts and even sell their property to do so (4:32–37).

At this point another aspect of the church's life appears. Ananias and Sapphira are struck dead because of their selfishness and hypocrisy (5:1–11). The apostles show their healing power and many believe the gospel (5:12–16). Again the apostles are arrested, but after being miraculously freed from prison, they are rearrested and then released after having been warned and beaten (5:17–42). The summarizing statement for this section is:

> And every day, in the temple and at home they did not cease teaching and preaching Jesus as the Christ (5:42).

B. The Spread in Judea, Samaria, Galilee and Damascus (6:1– 9:31)

These chapters (and similarly the next group) serve two functions. On the one hand, they describe the evangelization of Palestine outside of Jerusalem; on the other hand, they report bridges to the mission to the Gentiles. It will be noticed that half of the chapters in the present group are accounts of what happened in Jerusalem. But they introduce a significant new element. The Jews who stand on the foreground in chapters 6 and 7 are *Hellenist* Jews. Hellenists in this context were Jews who lived or had mainly lived in the Dispersion and used the Greek tongue. Their home was therefore among Gentiles (cf. 2:1–13). Chapter 8 introduces us to Saul who, known as Paul, became the great missionary of the early church. He was a Hellenist Jew, and chapter 9 relates his conversion.

A large number of Hellenist Jews in Jerusalem had become Christians. They complained that their Palestinian fellow-believers were not adequately caring for the needs of their widows (6:1). The "community of goods" was therefore not as complete as Luke's description would seem to indicate. The complaint led to the appointment of seven Hellenist Jewish Christians to assist in the daily distribution of food (6:2–7). One of these, Stephen, was a powerful evangelist. Hellenist Jews attacked his preaching, and he was brought before the council of Jewish leaders. This occasioned his long address with its severe indictment, which in turn led to his being stoned (7:1–58). It is this occasion that introduces Saul in the New Testament.

Stephen's death led to a persecution of the church. Many believers scattered and preached the gospel outside Jerusalem. Among them was Philip, one of the seven Hellenists appointed to care for the poor Hellenist widows. He preached in Samaria and converted an Ethiopean official returning from Jerusalem to his homeland (8:1–40). Then the account returns to Saul and relates his dramatic conversion on the road to Damascus, where he began his preaching ministry (9:1–30).

The summarizing sentence of this section is:

> So the church throughout all Judea and Galilee and Samaria had peace and was built up; and walking in the fear of the Lord and in the comfort of the Holy Spirit it was multiplied (9:31).

III. TRANSITION TO GENTILE MISSION (9:32– 12:25)

Gradually and very skillfully Luke completes the transition of gospel preaching from a purely Jewish to a predominantly Gentile situation. In the first group of chapters that we looked at the context is wholly Palestinian Jewish. Only Barnabas, a Hellenist Jew from Cyprus, is introduced. In the second section there is a very strong Hellenist Jewish presence, both believers and nonbelievers. In addition, we meet a Gentile, the Ethiopian eunuch. As a believer in the God of Israel, however, he stood in a close relationship to the Palestinian Jewish community. He is a very exceptional case, but he is presented as a Gentile who can be baptized.

In the present section two large steps are taken beyond the purely Jewish community, whether Palestinian or Hellenist. The first step involves Gentiles who are "God-fearers," that is, uncircumcised Gentile worshipers of the God of Israel. Here Peter is the preacher and active leader. The second step is an outreach to Gentiles who sustained no known relationship to the Jewish community at all. Here unknown believers first engage in a purely Gentile mission. Luke's approach to these far-reaching events is extremely careful and gradual. He places Peter in Lydda some twenty-five miles west of Jerusalem where he heals a lame man. He is then called to Joppa on the sea coast where he raises from the dead a woman, Dorcas, who was beloved by the community (9:32–43). Both situations are wholly Jewish, but they place Peter in a position from which the great transition from purely Jewish to wholly Gentile evangelism is to be made.

Twenty-seven miles north of Joppa lay Caesarea, the Roman capital of the Jewish province. It was a largely pagan city. Among its garrison there was a Roman centurion named Cornelius, a God-fearer. In a vision he is told to call Peter from Joppa. As this was happening, Peter had a preparatory vision of mixed clean and unclean animals lowered in a sheet from heaven, from which he is told to take, kill, and eat. When as a true Jew he protests against this, he hears the words, "What God has cleansed you must not call common" (10:1–16).

The next day Peter accompanies the men whom Cornelius had sent to call him. He meets with Cornelius and his believing Gentile friends, and sees the Holy Spirit descending upon them. Then Peter said, "Can anyone forbid water for baptizing these people, who have received the Holy Spirit just as we have?" When the elders in Jerusalem heard of this they called Peter to severe account. His report of the experience, however, witnessed as it had been by six believers whom he had brought along, convinced the elders of the rightness of his action: "Then to the Gentiles also God has granted repentance unto life" (10:17–11:18).

The reader is now ready for the final step that solidifies the massive Gentile mission that is shortly to be undertaken. Among the Jews who had left Jerusalem because of the persecution following Stephen's death were some Hellenist believers from Cyprus and Cyrene. These preached in Antioch to Greeks of whom no connections with Jews or Jewish Christians are reported. As the capital of the Roman province of Syria, Antioch was a large cosmopolitan city. Of the Greeks who heard the gospel "a great number that believed turned to the Lord." The barrier between Jew and Gentile had been finally broken. With this large and significant development came the realization—on whose part we do not know—that faith in Christ represented a new religion. Therefore "in Antioch the disciples were for the first time called Christians" (11:19–26).

At this point a shadow again falls on the progress of the gospel. Herod, the Roman-appointed king, unleashed a persecution against the leaders of the church in Jerusalem. He killed James the brother of John, and arrested Peter. But his life came to a tragic and humiliating end—in contrast to which stands the summarizing sentence of this section:

But the word of God grew and multiplied (12:24).

The way is now fully open for reporting the first church-sponsored mission to the Gentiles. The Jewish Christian has been led to surrender sole claim to the blessings of faith in Christ. The Gentile reader has been brought to see that Jesus is not the Savior of Jews only but of all people. With this understanding the reader, whether Jew or Greek, is prepared to accompany Paul on his mission to the Gentile world.

IV. *THE CHURCH AMONG THE GENTILES* (Paul)

A. The Spread Into Asia Minor (13:1– 16:5)

From the point of view of missionary practice this section is beyond question the most decisive and crucial part of the book of Acts. It is here that the power of the Holy Spirit as a universal witnessing force finds powerful expression in the practice of the church. The Holy Spirit can and does in specific instances act dramatically and once-for-all. The conversion of Paul is an outstanding example of this. But normally the Spirit chooses not so to act. He chooses rather to work within the framework of our life and history to bring us where he wants us to be. He works gradually, naturally, overcoming obstacles by his gentle power, leading and guiding the course of events to achieve his ends. The church's concern with the Hellenists in Jerusalem, the roles played by Stephen and Philip, Peter's vision of clean and unclean animals, the conversion of Cornelius and his household, the acknowledgment of Gentile salvation by the elders in Jerusalem, the preaching of the gospel by Hellenist Christians to Gentiles in Antioch, the preparation of Paul for missionary service—all this he caused to happen first. Then, with a broad background of Christian concern with the Gentiles on the record, he led the church officially to undertake the mission to the Gentiles and to validate this action by an apostolic council.

Similarly, the church had to *learn by experience* to go to the Gentiles. The tradition of Jewish privilege, the prejudices that this created, and the human reluctance to enter new paths were strong forces that had to be overcome. The command of Christ to preach the gospel to all men, beginning in Jerusalem, had been heard, it was known; but it was not comprehended, it was not understood. For this reason the command was not appropriated and made a part of the church's practice. Only when the church was, as it were, driven by its own experience to grasp the meaning of the command did it undertake the Gentile mission. This happened most decisively on Paul's first missionary journey when the Jews in Antioch of Pisidia in Asia Minor resisted the preaching of the gospel. It was then that Paul and Barnabas said,

> It was necessary that the word of God should be spoken first to you. Since you thrust it from you, and judge yourselves unworthy of eternal life, behold, we turn to the Gentiles (13:46, 47).

This did not mean the abandonment of the Jews; it did mean that the Gentiles have an equal right to the gospel. From this point on the church would have a double base—Gentile as well as Jewish.

Inevitably, this action would be challenged. On Paul's return to Antioch in Syria, Palestinian Jewish Christians, "believers who belonged to the party of the Pharisees," said that it was necessary to circumcise believing Gentiles and to hold them to the law of Moses (15:25). This meant, in short, that Gentiles had to become Jews in order to be members of the church. The council emphatically rejected this position, although it did request Gentile Christians to be considerate of Jewish views.

Hereupon Paul returned to Antioch and in due time delivered this decision to the churches that had been established on his first missionary journey. The summarizing statement for this section is:

> So the churches were strengthened in the faith, and they increased in numbers daily (16:5).

B. *ADVANCE INTO EUROPE* (16:6– 19:20)

We tend to divide the ministry of Paul into three missionary journeys and his journey to Rome. On the maps these are indicated by differently colored or differently stippled lines. While this is indeed helpful, it does not appear to be the way in which Luke regarded Paul's missionary service. One must read carefully to find the beginning of the third journey in 18:22, 23. The casual report on its beginning is reenforced by a break of five verses about Aquila, Priscilla, and Apollos (18:24–28). The summarizing or climactic statements with which the various sections of Acts close coincide only incidentally with the end of the journeys. The last statement we noted (16:5) appears in the course of the report on the second journey. The statement concluding the present section (19:20) occurs in the middle of the report on the third journey.

Each of the sections is governed, therefore, not by a journey idea but by a central theme. When this theme has been developed the summarizing statement concludes it. In this section the controlling thought is the entrance of the missionary proclamation into Europe.

In the light of history Paul's response to the Macedonian call (16:9, 10) was of profound significance. It is true that the gospel was already in Europe when Paul entered Macedonia. There was a church in Rome. But it lived there, as it were, on an island separated by more than 1,300 miles from the Christian home base in Jerusalem. Paul sought to bridge this gap. He had made an important beginning, perhaps unintentionally, in Asia Minor. The entrance into Europe was the beginning of an effort to evangelize the whole of Greece. When Luke has reported that this had measurably been done, his very next section (19:21–28:31) begins with Paul's expressed intention of completing the bridge. ". . . I must also see Rome." Some 650 years after Paul's entry into Europe, the Muslim armies conquered the whole arc curving from North Africa, Egypt, Palestine, and Syria to Asia Minor. For the next 1,200 years Europe was the chief custodian of the gospel.

The seventeenth chapter of Acts is a crucial one in the entire New Testament. Verses 16–34 relate Paul's encounter with the wise men of Greece. His preaching to them stands in marked contrast to Christian preaching in the Jewish community. In it the point of departure is the history of Israel (2:29ff.; 3:17ff.; 7:2ff.; 8:26ff.; 13:16ff.). Obviously Paul could not begin his preaching to the Gentiles with the history of Israel. They did not know it. He began, rather, with what all men have in common: religion and creation (vv. 22–28). In

Athens he did so in a specific and understandable way—he referred to the Athenian altar to the unknown god, and he quoted from their poets. His audience listened to him as one who knew what he was talking about. But this was only up to a point. Paul lost contact when he spoke about the resurrection of Christ. Here, in the judgment of his hearers, he departed from the common matters of religion and creation. The Greeks believed that life in the flesh is altogether inferior to a purely spiritual existence. To be rid of the body at death was gain. To desire to have it back seemed incomprehensible to them. "Now when they heard of the resurrection of the dead, some mocked, but others [more politely] said, 'We will hear you again about this' " (v. 32).

In Lystra (14:8–18) Paul had followed the same principle with a similar initial acceptance by the audience. There, however, his words had been a sudden response to a surprising situation. At Athens, Paul did not speak without preparation but with deliberate plan and purpose. Acts 17 provides the theological basis for all evangelistic witness to those who do not know the gospel.

This section also describes the beginning of Paul's association with two cities soon to play a large role in the life of the church, namely, Corinth and Ephesus. It may be noted, from the viewpoint of the relation between the church and the empire, that this provides a good illustration of the neutrality of the empire to Christianity. The proconsul Gallio would have nothing to do with a dispute between Jew and Christian (18:12–17). In the following section, 19:37 shows a similar attitude in Ephesus.

It should finally be noted that the divine prohibition to preach the gospel in Asia and Bithynia (16:6, 7) does not mean an exclusion of these areas from the hearing of the gospel. These were two Roman provinces in the eastern and northeastern part of what we call Asia Minor. The prohibition was temporary and was concerned only with missionary campaign strategy. At the end of the very same journey Paul briefly visited Ephesus, the largest and most important city in Asia. On his third journey he taught two years in Ephesus, "so that all the residents of Asia heard the word of the Lord, both Jews and Greeks" (19:10; cf. also I Peter 1:1). The concluding sentence of this section is:

So the word of the Lord grew and prevailed mightily (19:20).

C. Climax: The Gospel To Rome (19:21–28:31)
This section of nine and one-half chapters is longer than the two preceding sections together. In all three Paul is the central fig-

ure, but in 19:21–28:31 he holds the central role in a different way than in sections 13:1–16:5 and 16:6–19:20. The first two sections are distinctively missionary in character. In them Luke relates Paul's first and second missionary journeys and the larger part of his third and last. Although Paul the missionary is the central figure in the journey accounts, he is not the central fact in them. The central fact in 13:1–19:20 is clearly the tremendous expansion of the Christian faith in Asia Minor and Greece and the founding of the church in those areas. In the course of these travels Paul's major life work was done. In him, more than in any other, the gospel was established among the Gentiles and the foundations were laid for the worldwide church. When we consider the vast historic and redemptive significance of his work, Paul as the central figure in these sections is, in a sense, almost lost to sight.

In the section from 19:21 to the end of the book, it is not Paul the missionary but Paul the prisoner who is the central figure. There is in it no great central fact comparable to the founding of the church in Asia Minor and in Greece that tends to obscure the figure of Paul the prisoner. He has lost all ecclesiastical and missionary context. He is simply a Christian, taken prisoner by the Romans in a riot, moved from one place to another to escape death at the hands of enemies. Meanwhile, whether on land or at sea he gives sound and courageous witness to the faith that he proclaimed in his missionary labors. Finally, after perilous adventure, his travels come to an end when the centurion Julius, his gracious Roman guard, delivers him safely to the authority of the emperor.

Nevertheless, Acts 19:21–28:31 is more than an interesting bit of biography. In Luke's hand the journey becomes a symbol of the completion of Jesus' command, "You shall be my witnesses in Jerusalem and in all Judea and Samaria and to the end of the earth." Acts shows how Jerusalem, Judea, Samaria, and Gentile regions beyond Palestine were evangelized. The "end of the earth," Luke realized, would take a longer time to reach. But he would not permit this to keep the end of the earth out of his report. Therefore he made Rome, by which the whole of the then-known world was controlled, to be a symbol of the farthest reaches of the earth. As Jerusalem was the center from which all Judea and Samaria heard the gospel; as Ephesus was the center from which "all the residents of Asia heard the word of the Lord, both Jews and Greeks," so he viewed Rome, the great imperial capital, as the center from which the gospel would reach out to the entire world. To conquer Rome with the gospel would be the conquest of the world with the gospel.

As a powerless prisoner of the Roman world power and after a tempestuous life-threatening voyage, Paul reached the famed city. He arrived in weakness, with only some companions to be his community. Therefore when Roman brethren came to greet him he thanked God and took courage (28:15). He had completed his journey and reached his destination. The climax of this section and indeed of Acts as a whole is therefore found in these six simple words.

And so we came to Rome (28:14^b).

The task symbolically completed by Paul remains to be historically fulfilled by the church. This it continues to do in space and in time in the New Testament days of the End, under the imperative of the command of Christ and in the power of his Spirit.

PURPOSE

The overall theme of Acts is given in 1:8, "But you shall receive power when the Holy Spirit has come upon you; and you shall be my witnesses in Jerusalem and in all Judea and Samaria and to the end of the earth." One may almost say that the book works out this theme systematically. Chapters 2 to 12 deal with "Jerusalem, all Judea and Samaria"; chapters 13 to 28 with "to the end of the earth." The central figure in the first part is Peter; the central figure in the second part is Paul. The line dividing the Jewish and the Gentile missions is not, however, an altogether clearcut one. The preparation for the Gentile mission is laid in the area of the Jewish mission, that is, in chapters 1 to 12. The foundations for the Gentile mission are found in Jesus' command to preach the gospel worldwide (1:8), in the outpouring of the Spirit (2:1–13), in the conversion of the Ethiopean eunuch (8:26–40), in the conversion of Saul (9:1–25), in Peter's vision of clean and unclean creatures (10:9–16), in the conversion of Cornelius and his family (10:23–48), and in the preaching of the gospel to the Gentiles in Antioch (10:19–25). Similarly, the mission to the Gentiles, as is evident from Paul's missionary travels, did not ignore the Jews in the dispersion nor the needs and authority of the church in Jerusalem (13:13–52; 14:1–7; 16:11–15; 17:10–15; 18:1–7; 19:1–10; 22:1–23:11; 26:1–29, 28:17–28).

The inclusion of the Gentiles in the family of God, and the loss of Israel's priority, as the Jews had understood it, did not take place without struggle and pain. The way in which these changes took place illustrates the manner in which the Holy Spirit works in the church. His manner of working is one of gradualness, of naturalness, like development and growth in natural organisms. Teaching, tact, patience, gentleness, perseverance were needed to persuade the Jews of the demands of the gospel, and the Gentiles of their inclusion in its invitation. Pentecost sowed seeds, it did not plant full-grown trees. It gave the life of God's people a new direction, a broader scope, but the manner of achieving this had to be worked out in the life of the church. The understanding that the gospel was meant for Gentiles as well as Jews came into being slowly. It was a growth process, not a once-for-all event that brought into being this realization in the church.

We must also recognize the limits of the expression "the end of the earth" as Luke uses it. It is clear that in reaching Rome, Paul did not thereby reach the "end of the earth" in our understanding of the term. The expression has for us a predominantly geographical meaning, referring to unknown places far away. In the West this has been expressed by such terms as "foreign missions," "missions overseas," "the regions beyond." Undoubtedly Jesus had the geographic dimension in mind when he gave the Great Commission. Luke, however, adds to it a symbolic meaning. Rome was not the end of the earth, and it was not even the end of the Roman empire. Moreover, the gospel had already been established in Rome when Paul arrived there.

Nevertheless, Luke's "and so we came to Rome" (28:14[b]) is eloquent in the extreme. A foothold for the gospel had been found in the capital of the mightiest empire in the history of man. In Rome, soldiers, artists, traders, writers, and visitors from all corners of the empire and beyond it came and went in the pursuit of their purposes. The church established in Rome would be reaching the "ends of the earth" through travelers leaving and coming to Rome as well as through missionaries sent to the far corners of the then known world. Early Christianity was in fact urban-based, and from these urban centers the gospel spread into the surrounding regions. Therefore Paul could write to the church in Thessalonica, "not only has the word of the Lord sounded forth from you in Macedonia and Achaia, but your faith in God has gone forth everywhere . . ." (I Thess. 1:8). Luke may therefore well have envisioned the witness of the Roman church in the empire as a whole in the same way that Paul had seen Thessalonica related to Macedonia and Achaia.

In addition to his primary purpose of showing how Jesus' command to preach the gospel in the power of the Spirit had been carried out by the church, Luke also clearly had a secondary purpose in mind. It is identical with an important purpose that we noted in the discussion of Luke's gospel. Although he does not speak about it directly, his gospel gives evidence again and again of an effort to disarm the Roman authorities of any suspicions they might entertain with respect to the church and its faith. This theme is prominent throughout Acts.

Early on in his book Luke established a basic continuity between the gospel and the ancient faith of Israel (2:14ff.). This was important from a political point of view, for in the eyes of the Roman government Judaism was *religio licita*, that is, lawful religion. Christianity ought therefore to be accepted as a natural fulfillment or development of Israel's religion. The coming of the Holy Spirit, Luke points out, had been prophesied in the Old Testament (2:16), and the Messiah is a descendant of Israel's greatest king who had himself foretold the resurrection of Christ (2:25–36). We do not wish to suggest that Luke wrote chapter 2 of Acts with Roman officialdom primarily in mind. Peter's sermon was addressed to Jews. His words are fully understandable and justified from that fact alone. But his message is the basis for Paul's later defense of himself before the Roman authorities (24:10–21; 26:4–8, 22–23). Gallio, the Roman proconsul of Achaia, acknowledged earlier that Jewish charges against Paul concerned matters of Jewish law with which he had nothing to do (18:12–17). Luke stresses that Paul was a Roman citizen and therefore a privileged person (16:35–39; 21:39; 22:22–29; 25:10–12 [only Roman citizens could appeal to the emperor]). In addition, he tells us that Asiarchs, Romans of influence in the province of Asia, were among Paul's friends (19:28), and Roman officers guarding him are courteous and helpful (23:16–25; 27:3). Everywhere the Jews are blamed for Paul's sufferings and imprisonment and thereby the Roman authorities are excused from responsibility for them. Not least of all, Paul is allowed to have his own house while he is a prisoner in Rome, and he "lived at his own expense preaching the kingdom of God and teaching about the Lord Jesus Christ openly and unhindered" (28:30). From religious, social, civil, and judicial points of view, therefore, Luke presented Christianity and its chief spokesman in the Gentile world in a way that would dispose the Roman government to a friendly or at least a neutral attitude to the church and its message.

Luke's defense of Christianity would be all the more effective in the eyes of Roman readers because of its casual and incidental character. His aim to secure a favorable attitude to the gospel on the part of the Roman authorities may also explain the manner in

which the book ends. There is no report of Paul's death. It is altogether possible that Luke cut off his account of Paul's ministry
where he did so that he would not have to report Paul's execution
by the Roman government.

CHARACTERISTICS

In this section we consider certain features of Acts that are characteristic of it from beginning to end. Strictly speaking, the section
on the Holy Spirit in Acts belongs in this category of characteristics.
Because of its unusual importance, however, the entire final section
of this chapter will be devoted to that subject. Here we shall note
four features of significance: 1) the speeches in Acts, 2) the selective
character of the reporting, 3) the historical accuracy of Acts, and
4) the prominence of the resurrection theme.

1. *THE SPEECHES*

Luke reports sixteen speeches. However, there may be some
difference of opinion as to what constitutes a speech. In general we
distinguish between a conversation and a speech. The latter stands
in a formal context that the conversation does not have. For example, Jesus' words of farewell in chapter 1, however weighty, are
in the form of dialogue with his disciples and are therefore not
counted as a speech. The same is true of Paul's discussion with the
Jewish elders in Rome (28:17–20).

It is hardly to be supposed that the speeches (including ser-
mons) are verbatim reports of what was said. It was customary in
the Greek world to report speeches as the writer remembered them
or as they had been reported to him. In all probability both kinds
of reporting are found in Acts. Moreover, the speeches are almost
certainly condensed. They give the gist, the essence, of what the
speaker said. Peter's sermon in Acts 2 already suggests this. Luke
concludes his report on that address with, "And he testified with
many other words and he exhorted them, saying, 'Save yourselves
from this crooked generation' " (2:40). It is very unlikely that the
speech of the lawyer Tertullus to the governor consisted of only the
six verses 24:2–8, or Paul's defense of only ten verses, 24:10–21.
This does not mean that the reporting was inaccurate or inadequate;
it does mean that it does not include all that was said.

Most of the speeches are sermonic in character. As such they
present a good idea of the content of the earliest preaching. The
prominence of Jesus' resurrection is noteworthy. The resurrection

references presuppose, of course, Jesus' death, and that may be the reason for the lesser emphasis on his death. It may not be forgotten that the same person who wrote Acts wrote also the gospel with its account of the passion of Christ. Most of the references to the crucifixion in Acts stand in a context of rebuke to the Jews for their criminal action. Jesus' death as a saving act is not prominent in the book. It may well be that the power of Easter and Pentecost pressed the cross into the background. Paul's letters, written at least fifteen years before Acts, present Jesus' cross, death, resurrection, ascension, and session at the right hand of the Father as also the work of the Holy Spirit, in their full inter-relationships.

The speeches in Acts follow below. They reward reading and rereading. Five are by Peter, six by Paul, and one each by Gamaliel, Stephen, James, the lawyer Tertullus, and a spokesman of the Jerusalem elders to Paul.

2:14–40	Peter	Pentecost sermon
3:12–26	Peter	sermon in Solomon's porch
4:8–12	Peter	defense before the Sanhedrin
5:34–39	Gamaliel	exhortation to caution to the Sanhedrin
7:1–53	Stephen	address to and rebuke of the Sanhedrin
10:34–43	Peter	sermon to Cornelius' household
11:5–17	Peter	defense in Jerusalem
13:16–41	Paul	sermon in Antioch of Pisidia
15:13–21	James	to apostolic council in Jerusalem
17:22–31	Paul	on the Areopagus in Athens
20:18–35	Paul	farewell to Ephesian elders
21:20–25	Jerusalem elders to Paul	
22:1–21	Paul	defense in Jerusalem
24:2–8	Tertullus	contra Paul
24:10–21	Paul	reply to Tertullus
26:2–29	Paul	defense before Agrippa

2. SELECTIVE REPORTING

Like the gospels, Acts is selective in its reporting. In his own way and in the context of the Holy Spirit working in the church, Luke could have concluded his account as John did his gospel in 20:30, 31. Acts is not, and therefore must not be viewed, as a more or less comprehensive history of the first thirty years of the church's life. The key to the understanding of Acts is 1:8; "But you shall receive power when the Holy Spirit has come upon you; and you shall be my witnesses in Jerusalem and in all Judea and Samaria and to the end of the earth." This is the theme that Luke develops in his book.

The history reported in Acts centers around the leading figure of Peter for the area designated as "Jerusalem, all Judea and Samaria," and around another leading figure, Paul, for the area designated as "the end of the earth." Within these areas, only certain places are selected to report on. In the former area these are Jerusalem, Samaria, Lydda, Joppa, Caesarea; in the latter are Antioch, a number of cities in Asia Minor and Greece, along with Paul's journey to Rome. To show the movement of the gospel from Jerusalem to Rome in the power of the Spirit is Luke's aim. For this reason we hear almost nothing concerning the work of the other ten apostles, about the spread of the gospel to other areas, about many experiences of Paul related in his letters, or concerning other agents and methods of gospel proclamation. Who can say in how many areas and different ways the kind of evangelism reported in 11:20, 21 was repeated? The principle underlying the reporting of the speeches was equally operative in the writing of Acts as a whole.

3. *HISTORICAL RELIABILITY*

Modern students of Acts have been surprised at the accuracy of Luke's reporting. The British scholar Sir William Ramsay has demonstrated this through his researches in Asia Minor. He has shown that names, places, titles, routes of travel, customs, and the like have all been used or alluded to in Acts in conformity with facts and usage existing during the thirty years covered by Acts. In view of this, however, some problems arise of which we should take note. Nowhere in Acts does Luke refer to Paul's letters, although some of them were written when Luke was with Paul (Col. 4:14; II Tim. 4:11; Philemon 24). All of them were written at least twenty years before Luke wrote Acts. How must we account for lack of any reference to them in Acts? A further and related problem lies in the inability of New Testament scholars to harmonize data in Acts about Paul's visits to Jerusalem with those that Paul himself reports in his letter to the Galatians. The references in Acts are to four distinct visits: 9:26–30; 11:30 and 12:25; 15:1–35; and 21:1–19. In addition, a number of scholars understand the words "he went up and greeted the church" (18:22) to refer to a fifth visit. But the references in Galatians are to two visits: 1:18–24 and 2:1–10. The difficulty here lies not so much in the difference between four (or five) visits in Acts and only two in Galatians, as in relating the two visits mentioned in Galatians to particular visits reported in Acts. We shall not attempt to do here what the most expert scholarship extending over many years, and expressing itself in various carefully argued theories, has been unable to do. We will limit ourselves to two observations:

a) Luke began his gospel with these words:

Inasmuch as many have undertaken to compile a narrative of the things which have been accomplished among us, just as they were delivered to us by those who from the beginning were eyewitnesses and ministers of the word, it seemed good to me also, having followed all things closely for some time past, to write an orderly account for you, most excellent Theophilus. . . .

Since Acts is most intimately related to the gospel as a sequel to it, was written by the same author, and dedicated to the same Theophilus, there is no reason to question that the manner in which Luke describes his writing of the gospel applies equally to his writing of Acts. This is borne out by the accuracy we have noted with respect to matters on which it is possible to test his reliability. Luke's carefulness in writing does not, however, come to expression in forms more or less equivalent to modern scientific techniques of footnotes, page references, bibliographies, dates, and the like. He was careful in the only way in which he could be careful, namely, in accord with the literary norms that governed responsible writers of his time.

b) As we noted in discussing the Synoptics and John, the writers of New Testament history were in the first place concerned with the presentation of a message. They stand in one line with the writers of Joshua, Judges, Samuel, and Kings, who in the Hebrew Bible are not called historians but "the Former Prophets," as Isaiah, Jeremiah, Ezekiel, and the minor prophets Hosea to Malachi are called "the Latter Prophets." The framework of data, sequence, evidence, and form to which so much attention is paid in the biblical scholarship of our time did not so dominate the writing of the prophetic message of the Bible.

With respect to Paul's visits to Jerusalem, therefore, we do not know how fully either he or Luke reported his movements at any given time. Each reported only as much as he deemed to be relevant to the message that he expressed in his writing. Luke's nonreference to Paul's letters must be seen in the same light. There is no reason to believe that Luke was unaware of the letters that Paul had written; there is as little cause to believe that for one reason or another he ignored them. What is probably of more importance than either of these unlikely possibilities is the fact that Paul was living during the whole period concerning which Luke wrote. So long as Paul was able to travel, to write, and to speak, his letters in all probability had only local meaning for the church—the letters to the Corinthians in Corinth, to the Colossians in Colossae, to Titus and Philemon in their respective lives. Moreover, Paul doubtless wrote more letters, perhaps many more, than those we now have. We know that only one of these, a letter to the Laodiceans, was shared with another congregation, the church in Colossae (Col. 4:16). It was after his death that certain of his letters gradually became the inheritance of the church as a whole. For these reasons, we judge, such questions are not significant, nor their answers necessary, for a genuine understanding of the message of Acts. In view of the reliability of the data that Luke adduces in Acts, such considerations would seem to justify holding in suspension a judgment on the number of visits Paul made to Jerusalem.

4. *THE RESURRECTION THEME*

A very striking characteristic of Acts is its emphasis on resurrection. Thirteen times it speaks about the resurrection of Jesus, eight about resurrection in general but even then in connection with the resurrection of Jesus. The passages referring to Christ's resurrection are: 1:3, 22; 2:24, 31, 32; 3:15, 26; 4:10, 33; 5:30; 10:40; 13:30–37; 17:18, 31. References to resurrection in general are 4:2; 17:18, 22; 23:6, 8; 24:15, 21; 26:8. This stands in sharp contrast to the relatively few references to the crucifixion. In these the crucifixion is presented mainly as a crime committed by the Jews (2:23, 24; 3:13, 15; 4:10; 5:30; 7:52, 56; 13:28, 31). Directly over against this sinful act stands, in every instance, the act of God raising Jesus from the dead, except in 7:52–56 where the resurrection is implied.

This priority of the redemptive theme of resurrection is not accidental. The earlier part of Acts deals with the time immediately following the resurrection of Jesus. This event powerfully impressed the disciples, and it became the theme of Christian preaching. In the second place, resurrection occupies a weighty place in two samples given of Paul's preaching. One of these is taken from his preaching to Jews (13:30–37), the other from his preaching to Gentiles (17:30–32). This is not surprising, since the resurrection theme is a cornerstone in the structure of Paul's theology as set forth in his letters.

THE HOLY SPIRIT IN ACTS

The account that records the Pentecost event in Acts 2 bears a strange and unusual character. Few people, even those in the ministry, know how it should be understood. It is therefore seldom preached on, except in a general way that does little with the specific facts of the account. Everything is allowed to remain mysterious.

This contributes to a view of the Holy Spirit as a power that leads many Christians into peculiar beliefs and conduct. But that is hardly in keeping with Paul's instruction to the Corinthian church in connection with the gifts of the Holy Spirit. Referring especially to the gift of speaking with tongues he said, "So, my brethren, earnestly desire to prophesy, and do not forbid speaking in tongues, but all things should be done decently and in order" (I Cor. 14:39, 40). A brief explanation of Acts 2:1–13 will show that the Holy Spirit does not deserve to be associated with confusion and abnormal behavior, but rather with the fundamental structure of the church of Christ. We shall see that there is indeed mystery in the Pentecost event but, like creation, it is an eminently ordered and fruitful mystery.

The word *pentekoste* is Greek, meaning "fiftieth." As the name of a feast Pentecost was an Old Testament harvest festival celebrated on the fiftieth day (or seven weeks) after the Passover. It is therefore in the Old Testament also called the Feast of Weeks. On the particular day of Pentecost described in Acts 2, followers of Jesus, "about a hundred and twenty" in number (1:15), were "all together in one place" (2:1). To them the Holy Spirit revealed himself by three notable signs. That is to say, the Holy Spirit did not just "come" to the church on Pentecost. He came to indwell it in a certain manner. If this *manner* of his coming is taken out of the Pentecost event there is no Pentecost event left. The signs of his coming indicate the meaning and nature of his coming. In the course of their meeting together the disciples suddenly heard a sound like the rushing of a mighty wind, and they saw tongues like fire resting on each one of them. These two signs were immediately followed by a third. Spontaneously, they began to speak in other languages "the mighty works of God" (2:12).

The character and the relationship of these signs to each other should be noted carefully. The signs of the wind and of the fire did not come in the form of actual wind and fire. There was a *sound* of wind, but no wind itself; and there were tongues *like* fire, but there was no actual fire. They were, therefore, exclusively symbolic appearances. The speaking in tongues, on the other hand, is presented by Luke as *an actual speaking*, a witness, a preaching in words that were clearly understood and in languages that were actually being spoken at that time in various parts of the Roman empire. As symbols, however, the wind and fire are important. Wind speaks of might and power. How fearfully strong a storm, much more a tornado, can be. And as fire purifies and gives light, it stands together with the wind as symbol of the Spirit's effect and power. But it is on the

actual speaking in tongues that the overwhelming emphasis falls in
the Pentecost account. The symbol of the sound of wind is mentioned in verse 2 and not again; the symbol of the tongues like fire
is mentioned in the third verse, but it also is not again referred to.
The speaking in tongues, however, receives the attention of all the
remaining verses, and it is in various ways elaborated both in the
account itself and in the sermon of Peter that immediately follows.
The function of the appearance of wind and fire stands supportively
and reenforcingly in the background, but the center of interest and
importance lies clearly in the speaking. We must therefore look into
this happening to find the central meaning of Pentecost.

As a result of sundry causes hundreds of thousands of Jews
lived outside of Palestine. Many who went into exile in Babylon
never returned. Others were expatriated as a result of capture or
enslavement in war. Still others went out as traders and stayed to
live and work in one country or another. This spreading out of the
Jews throughout the entire Roman world and beyond is known as
the Jewish Dispersion. In it, however, they retained their religion
and their love for the land of their fathers. Every year many visited
their traditional homeland, and the Passover Feast was a favorite
time for doing so. Often they stayed long enough to be present also
at the Feast of Pentecost. It was for this reason that so many Jews
from other countries were present in Jerusalem when the church
experienced its Pentecost drama. No less than fifteen countries or
regions are mentioned in the list of nations given in 2:9–11.

There were no Gentile recipients of the Holy Spirit. The entire
preparation of the gospel from Abraham to Jesus' ascension to heaven
took place within the confines of Israel. Luke, however, seeing so
many Jews from distant countries hearing the message of the gospel,
regarded these Dispersion Jews as representatives of the Gentile
"ends of the earth" who would one day embrace the Word of life.

The *speaking* of the gospel in the languages of *many nations* is
a double symbol of profound significance for understanding the
character and purpose of the church of Christ. The speaking in
tongues (languages) to people from all parts of the Roman empire
declared the church to be a *witnessing* and a *universal* body. On this
Pentecost day the Holy Spirit became an integral and abiding part
of the organization and life of the people of God as he had never
been before. Through him the church became a speaking, teaching,
and preaching church. The preacher took the place of the priest, the
pulpit took the place of the altar; preaching and service that of
sacrifice; and the Christian assembly for worship that of synagogue

and temple. Thus was Jesus' promise fulfilled, "You shall *be* my witnesses. . . ." That is to say, preaching, teaching, and witnessing are not activities of the church alongside of many others. It is the essential nature and being of the church to preach, to teach, to evangelize. These are not simply things that it *does*; the doing of these things is what it *is*. The Old Testament expectation of messianic-event-to-come was superseded by the proclamation of messianic-event-accomplished. With it the symbolism of temple, sacrifice, priest, and altar disappeared, and in their place came the church of Christ with preaching and sacrament as its central service.

On the same day and through the same cause, the church became a universal body. It spread from Jerusalem and Judea to stand and serve literally at the ends of the earth. The church is a worldwide body, an ecumenical body. It knows no national, tribal, or linguistic boundaries. On Pentecost the Holy Spirit at long last destroyed the curse of Babel where language divided and scattered men (Gen. 11:1–9). On Pentecost language as bearer of "the mighty works of God" reconciled and reunited men. There the great outward movement of the witnessing church began, and in its power the movement continues to this day.

It is true that this great change-over in the life of the people of God from Old Testament forms and spirit to New Testament forms and spirit was not immediately understood and did not immediately become fully evident. Acts shows plainly how difficult it was for the disciples to accept this new way of the Spirit. Indeed, the change took many years to take hold and become effective. Foundations were laid, however, on which the universal church could be built. Acts leads us through the earliest Jewish and Gentile history of the new era that had dawned in the life of the people of God. Therein lies the central character of the book.

It is therefore understandable that of the five historical books with which the New Testament begins, Acts makes by far the most extensive reference to the Holy Spirit. We meet him repeatedly at crucial moments in the history that Acts relates. Such occasions are: Jesus' command to preach the gospel worldwide beginning from Jerusalem (1:8); the coming of the Spirit (2:1–9); the large initial ingathering of 3,000 (2:33–38); the judgment on Ananias and Saphira (5:1–11); Stephen's rebuke of the Jewish leaders (7:51); the conversion of the Ethiopian eunuch (8:39); the conversion of Cornelius and his house (10:47, 11:28); the appointment of Saul and Barnabas as the first missionaries to the Gentiles (13:2); the official admission of Gentiles into the church (15:8, 28); the entrance of the gospel into

Europe (16:6); the baptism of Apollos and his friends (19:1–7); the task of elders in the church (20:28); and the relation of the gospel to Jews and Gentiles (28:25–28).

All in all, it is understandable that many students of Acts have suggested that the book might more appropriately have been called the Acts of the Holy Spirit.